Great Letters in American History

GREAT
LETTERS
* * * * * * * IN * * * * * * *
AMERICAN
HISTORY

WORDS FROM THE PENS OF AMERICANS—
GREAT AND SMALL

REBECCA PRICE JANNEY

HORIZON BOOKS

CAMP HILL, PENNSYLVANIA

HORIZON BOOKS

3825 Hartzdale Drive, Camp Hill, PA 17011
www.cpi-horizon.com

Great Letters in American History
ISBN: 0-88965-158-2
LOC Catalog Card Number: 99-080155

00   01   02   03   04   5   4   3   2   1

Unless otherwise indicated,
Scripture taken from the HOLY BIBLE:
NEW INTERNATIONAL VERSION ®
Copyright © 1973, 1978, 1984 by the
International Bible Society. Used by
permission of Zondervan Bible Publishers.

Dedication

For David Fessenden, who inspired this book
and encourages me to share and develop my
historical knowledge to the glory of God.

Contents

Acknowledgments

I owe my thanks to many people for their contributions to this book, from Jennifer Womer, my Lafayette College friend and "ex-tern," who helped me locate correspondence at the start of this project, to Joanna Hause and Ruth Meyer of Biblical Theological Seminary for their assistance in locating books, to Bernice Kemmler, for bringing to my attention the letter from "The Civil War" and for her unfailing cheerfulness and dedication in making my public speaking engagements so much easier and enjoyable.

Many people also assisted me in finding letters related to their libraries, foundations and memorials. I would like to thank Thomas E. Camden of the George C. Marshall Foundation, Herbert L. Pankratz and Dan Holt of the Dwight D. Eisenhower Library, and Mr. John S.D. Eisenhower for permission to use his father's letters; Lana Henry of the George Washington Carver National Monument; Rosie Atherton from the John Fitzgerald Kennedy Library; Glenn A. Walsh of the Andrew Carnegie Free Library; and Raymond Teichman, Supervisory Archivist at the Franklin D. Roosevelt Library.

Also, thanks to Doris Secor for sending me a nineteenth-century book about great women of that day.

Finally, I thank God for giving me another opportunity to share with my fellow Americans the special way in which He has raised up people throughout our history to glorify Him and better the lives of others, and for providing my husband, Scott, who is a constant source of love and encouragement to me.

Introduction

During the Christmas season of 1966 the local paper ran an article asking people to send Christmas cards to area servicemen and women in Vietnam. Something about the appeal stirred my soul, and I asked my mother to help me send two cards. I was eight years old. The two soldiers answered the letters I included with the season's greetings, and we began a lengthy correspondence. Although it lasted two or more years until both came home safely, I no longer have copies of their letters or the pictures they sent me. Nor can I fully understand why we never arranged to meet each other when the soldiers returned.

Nevertheless, that experience left a lasting impression on me; those men told me how much my letters meant to them. I can only imagine how special a childish, innocent letter containing Peanuts® comic strips must have meant to world-weary soldiers fighting a war that few people understood. I know that I came to cherish their letters and have developed an enduring appreciation for correspondence, especially the heart-warming kind. It still thrills me when I open a chintz-covered hatbox containing letters my husband and I have written to each other since we met in 1981.

American history is like a huge old hatbox full of wonderful letters between people who used those opportunities to share with each other what God meant in their lives. These include correspondence between husbands and wives, statesmen and their peers, military leaders and their admirers, politicians and their detractors, scientists and their followers.

I read some of them with tears in my eyes: the touching letter of Civil War soldier Sullivan Ballou and the poignant public disclosure to the American people of Ronald Reagan's Alzheimer's diagnosis. Most of them lifted my spirits and encouraged me to share their messages with my readers so that they too might see the hand of God at work around them.

This work is by no means exhaustive. In fact I have a great sense of unfinished business. The more I read, the more I realized how vast was the task of choosing just a few of the great letters that are out there. Obviously, many great Americans are not included in this collection due to time and space limitations.

Like my previous book, *Great Stories in American History*, not all of these letters were written by

Introduction

Christian men and women. Instead, each letter
conveys in some sense the work of God in the
American experience. Though arranged in chapters
covering various periods of American history, a top-
ical index is included so that you may read them either sequentially or according to how the various
themes relate to your needs of the moment. I find it
tremendously inspiring to find out how exemplary
Americans faced life's many moods and seasons, in
their own words.

My prayer for you is that as you read *Great Letters in
American History* you will find wisdom and encouragement for your soul, even as you are drawn into a closer
fellowship with the Author behind their inspiration.
This is the God who chose to write letters to His children through the inspired thoughts of His chosen
scribes. May this book be an appetizer to the feast
that awaits you in those epistles.

Rebecca Price Janney

Some Notations of Style

These letters appear exactly in the form in which I
found them, including oddities of style, grammar
and punctuation, in order to convey their closest
meaning and to more accurately reflect the times
and circumstances in which they were written.
Sometimes this presents a special challenge to the
reader, as in the case of Sarah Sinons. That young
Native American used precious little punctuation in
her letters.

I didn't always have the writer's salutation or closings, and in a few cases, I constructed my own based on their other correspondence or according to the standard form of their times.

To the best of my ability I have preserved the original words and intent of these letter writers.

Rather than using footnotes or endnotes to identify my sources, I have put the authors and page numbers in brackets at the end of each letter, and included every published source in a bibliography.

I

The New World:
Letters of the Colonial Period

Wнат мотіvated тне explorers who crossed an uncharted ocean to a mysterious new land? What kind of people were the first settlers on American soil?

The letters that follow give a unique glimpse into the early history of our country.

"So great a victory and gift"

Genoa-born Christopher Columbus (1451-1506) went to sea when he was fourteen years old. Shipwrecked in Portugal on that first voyage, Columbus settled there. Later, he tried to secure support for a trip to India via the West from the Portuguese crown. That denied, Columbus turned to Spain's Ferdinand and Isabella to finance the journey.

In 1493, the year after his discovery of the "New World," Columbus wrote to Gabriel Sanchez, King Ferdinand's treasurer. In his descriptions of the native peoples he met, the admiral emphasized his desire that they come to know Christ. This important feature of his motivation in seeking new lands often is ignored in favor of the view that he was pursuing personal wealth and Spanish glory alone.

"Let Christ rejoice on earth, as he rejoices in heaven, when he foresees coming to salvation so many souls of people hitherto lost."

In all these islands there is no difference in the appearance of the people, nor in the manners and language, but all understand each other mutually; a fact that is very important for the end which I suppose to be earnestly desired by our most illustrious king, that is, their conversion to the holy religion of Christ, to which in truth, as far as I can perceive, they are very ready and favorably inclined. . . .

7

In all these islands, as I have understood, each man is content with only one wife, except the princes of kings, who are permitted to have twenty. The women appear to work more than the men. I was not able to find out surely whether they have individual property, for I saw that one man had the duty of distributing to the others, especially refreshments, food, and things of that kind. . . .

Truly great and wonderful is this, and not corresponding to our merits, but to the holy Christian religion, and to the piety and religion of our sovereigns, because what the human understanding could not attain, that the divine will has granted to human efforts. For God is wont to listen to his servants who love his precepts, even in impossibilities, as has happened to us on the present occasion, who have attained that which hitherto mortal men have never reached.

For if anyone has written or said anything about these islands, it was all with obscurities and conjectures; no one claims that he had seen them; from which they seemed like fables. Therefore let the king and queen, the princes and their most fortunate kingdoms, and all other countries of Christendom give thanks to our Lord and Saviour Jesus Christ, who has bestowed upon us so great a victory and gift. Let religious processions be solemnized; let sacred festivals be given; let the churches be covered with festive garlands. Let Christ rejoice on earth, as he rejoices in heaven, when he foresees coming to salvation so many souls of people hitherto lost. Let us be glad also, as well on account of the exaltation of our faith, as on account of the increase of our temporal affairs, of which not only

Spain, but universal Christendom will be partaker. These things that have been done are thus briefly related. Farewell, Lisbon, the day before the ides of March.

Christopher Columbus,
admiral of the Ocean fleet
[Schuster, pp. 67-68]

"I made declaration of the contents of the Bible"

Thomas Harriot (1560-1621), English-born and Oxford-trained, became Sir Walter Raleigh's mathematical tutor in 1581, a position he held for four years. A year later he ventured across the ocean to Virginia in order to survey that strange and wonderful place.

In 1588 Harriot set out to write a "brief and true report of the new found land of Virginia" to all those English patrons and enthusiasts interested in establishing a British colony in the New World. Actually, the "brief and true" letter was quite lengthy, running to several dozen pages. In these excerpts he discussed the impact of the gospel on some of the Native Americans he encountered, a topic of considerable importance to this man who came to the New World not to glorify his adventurous spirit or the Crown of England, but Almighty God.

"The Wiroans [chief] with whome we dwelt called Wingina, and many of his people would be glad many times to be with us at our prayers. . . ."

To the gentle Reader, wisheth all hapinesse in the Lord.

Albeit (gentle Reader) the credite of the reports in this treatise contained, can litle be furthered by the testimonie of one as my selfe, through affection judged partiall, though without desert: Neverthelesse, forsomuch as I have bene requested by some my particular friends, who conceive more rightly of me, to deliver freely my knowledge of the same, not onely for the satisfying of them, but also for the true information of any other who soever, that comes not with a prejudicate minde to the reading thereof: Thus much upon my credite I am to affirme, that things universally are so truely set downe in this treatise by the authour thereof, an Actor in the Colonie and a man no lesse for his honestie then learning commendable, as that I dare boldly avouche, it may very well passe with the credite of trueth even amongst the most true relations of this age. Which as for mine owne part I am readie any way with my worde to acknowledge, so also (of the certaintie thereof assured by mine owne experience) with this my publique assertion, I doe affirme the same. Farewell in the Lord. . . .

Since the first undertaking by Sir Walter Raleigh to deale in the action of discovering of that Countrey which is now called and knowen by the name of Virginia, many voiages having bene thither made at sundry times to his great charge, as first in the yeere 1584, and afterwards in the yeeres 1585, 1586, and now of late this last yeere of 1587. There have been divers and variable reportes, with some slanderous and shamefull speaches bruited abroad by many that returned from thence. . . . Which reports have not done a little wrong to many that otherwise would have also favoured and adventured in the action, to the honour and benefite of our nation, besides the particular profite and credite which would redound to themselves the dealers therein, as I hope by the sequell of events to the shame of those

that have avouched the contrary shall be manifest, if
you the adventurers, favourers and welwillers doe
but either increase in number, or in opinion continue, or having bene doubtfull, renew your good
liking and furtherance to deale therein according to
the woorthiness thereof alreadie found, and as you
shall understand heerafter to be requisite. . . .

I have therefore thought it good beying one that
have bene in the discoverie, and in dealing with the
naturall inhabitaunts specially imployed: and having therefore seene and knowen more then the
ordinarie, to impart so much until you of the fruits
of our labours, as that you may know how injuri-
ously the enterprise is slaundered, and that in
publique maner at this present. . . .

Many times and in every towne where I came, according as I was able, I made declaration of the con-
tents of the Bible, that therein was set foorth the
true and onely God, and his mightie workes, that
therein was conteined the true doctrine of salvation
through Christ, with many particularities of Miracles and chiefe pointes of Religion, as I was able
then to utter, and thought fit for the time. And although I tolde them the booke materially and of it
selfe was not of any such vertue, as I thought they
did conceive, but onely the doctrine therein
conteined; yet woulde many bee glad to touche it,
to embrace it, to kisse it, to holde it to their breastes
and heades, and stroke over all their body with it, to
shewe their hungrie desire of that knowledge which
was spoken of.

The Wiroans [chief] with whome we dwelt called
Wingina, and many of his people would be glad

many times to be with us at our prayers, and many times call upon us both in his owne towne, as also in others whither he sometimes accompanied us, to pray and sing Psalmes, hoping thereby to be partaker of the same effects which we by that meanes also expected.

Twise this Wiroans was so grievously sicke that hee was like to die, and as he lay languishing, doubting of any helpe by his owne priestes, and thinking he was in such danger for offending us, and thereby our God, sent for some of us to pray and bee a meanes to our God that it woulde please him either that hee might live, or after death dwell with him in blisse, so likewise were the requests of many others in the like case.

On a time also when their corne began to wither by reason of a drought which happened extraordinarily, fearing that it had come to passe by reason that in some thing they had displeased us, many would come to us and desire us to pray to our God of England, that hee woulde preserve their corne, promising that when it was ripe we also should be partakers of the fruite.

There coulde at no time happen any strange sickenesse, losses, hurtes, or any other crosse until them, but that they woulde impute to us the cause or meanes thereof, for offending or not pleasing us.

One other rare and strange accident, leaving other, will I mention before I ende, which mooved the whole Countrey that either knewe or heard of us, to have us in wonderful admiration.

There was no towne where we had any subtile devise practise against us, we leaving it unpunished or

not revenged (because we sought by all meanes possible to win them by gentlenesse) but that within a
fewe dayes after our departure from every such
towne, the people began to die very fast, and many
in short space, in some townes about twentie, in
some fourtie, and in one six score, which in trueth
was very many in respect of their nombers. This
happened in no place that we could learne, but
where we had bene, where they used some practise
against us, and after such time. The disease also so
strange, that they neither knew what it was, nor how
to cure it, the like by report of the oldest men in the
Countrey never happened before, time out of
minde. A thing specially observed by us, as also by
the natural inhabitants themselves.

Insomuch that when some of the inhabitants which
were our friends, and especially the Wiroans Wingina,
had observed such effects in foure or five townes to
followe their wicked practises, they were perswaded
that it was the worke of our God through our meanes,
& that we by him might kil and slay whom we would
without weapons, and not come neere them.

And thereupon when it had happened that they
had understanding that any of their enemies had
abused us in our journeys, hearing that we had
wrought no revenge with our weapons, and fearing
upon some cause the matter should so rest: did
come and intreate us that wee woulde be a meanes
to our God that they as others that had dealt ill with
us might in like sort die, alleadging how much it
would be for our credite and profite, as also theirs,
and hoping furthermore that we would doe so much

at their requests in respect of the friendship we professed them. . . .

[Quinn, pp.46-47, 70-72]

"Dear in my thoughts"

A group of distinguished Cambridge University alumni gathered in late summer 1629 to sign an agreement that they would emigrate to New England sometime within the next seven months. Among their many tasks was to elect a governor. They chose lawyer John Winthrop (1588-1649), a man of prosperity who decided to risk it all on a divinely appointed experiment. The Puritans went to New England not for material or personal gain, but to establish in New England "a city upon a hill" for all the world to see and by which to gain inspiration and salvation. In March, 1630, Winthrop departed England with one son on the flagship Arbella. He left behind his wife and son, John Jr., who would later join him in the New World.

A common, but false, assumption is that Puritan men and women were dour individuals for whom laughter and joy were not only foreign but forbidden, that a cool aloofness defined their relationships. Quite the opposite is the case, as evidenced by the following letters written by Winthrop and his wife, Margaret, over several years. Through this tender correspondence comes the clear message that God and His will must take precedence in their affections.

"My sweet spouse, let us delight in the love of each other as the chief of all earthly comfort . . ."

To my loving friend Mrs. Winthrop at Chelmsly House in Great Maplested, Exxes.

My Dear Wife,
I beseech the Lord of good God to bless thee and thy little babe with all spiritual blessings in heavenly things, and with a comfortable supply of all things needful for this present life, with such a portion of the true wisdom as may cause us always to discern of the worth & excellency of Christ Jesus, to take him as our onely portion, & to love him with all our heart, as our best thank offering for his unspeakable love & mercy in redeeming us from our sins by his own death, & adopting us into the right of the inheritance of his father's Kingdom. To him be glory & praise for ever, Amen.

Albeit I cannot conveniently come to thee yet, I could not but send to know how thou doest, & in what state thy good mother continueth, with the rest of our friends: That which we now forsee & fear in her, we must look to come to ourselves, & then neither friends nor goods, pleasure nor honor, will stand us in any stead, onely a good conscience sprinkled with the blood of Christ shall give us peace with God & our own souls.

We are all here in good health (I praise God) yet not well contented until thou returnest to Groton, but I will not hasten to abridge thy dear mother of that comfort which she may receive in thy company. My sweet spouse, let us delight in the love of each other as the chief of all earthly comfort: & labor to increase therein by the constant experience of each other's faithfulness & sincerity of affection, formed into the similitude of the Love of Christ and his Church. Look for me on Thursday or Friday (if God will) & remember me to thy good mother & all the rest, as thou knowest my duty & desires, etc. My parents salute thee; many kisses of Love I send thee: farewell.

John Winthrop
July 12, 1620 (Groton)

Most dear & loving Wife,—I wrote unto thee by our neighbor Cole, being then uncertain of my return, yet I hoped to have been with thee on Saturday but it so falleth out, that I am enforced to stay except I should leave my sister Goldings destitute, & the business I came for without effect, which I cannot now fail with comfort & good report. Therefore I must entreat thy gentle patients until this business be dispatched, which I hope will be by the next week. In the mean time thou art well persuaded that my heart is with thee, and (I know) thine is with him to whom thou has given thyself, a faithful & loving yokefellow: who truly prizing this gift as the greatest earthly blessing, provokes the Love to abound in those fruits of mutual kindness, etc., that many add a daily increase of comfort & sweet content in this happiness. I would willingly offer a request unto thee, which yet I will not urge (not knowing what inconveniences may lie in the way), but it would be very grateful to me to meet thee at Maplested on Wednesday next, but be it as God shall guide thy heart & the opportunity. It is now near XI of the clock & time to sleep, therefore I must end. The Lord of heavenly father bless & keep thee & all ours, & let this salutation serve for all, for I know not how safe a messenger I shall have for these. Remember my duty & Love as thou knowest how to bestow them.

> Farewell,
> Thine John Winthrop
> I send these divers things by
> Wells in a trusse.
> May 10, 1621
> (London)

Dear in my thoughts,—I blush to think how much I have neglected the opportunity of presenting my love to you. Sad thoughts possess my spirits, and I cannot repulse them; which makes me unfit for any thing, wondering what the Lord means by all these troubles among us. Sure I am, that all shall work to the best of them that love God, or rather are loved of him. I know he will bring light out of obscurity, and make his righteousness shine forth as the noon day. Yet I find in myself an adverse spirit, and a trembling heart, not so willing to submit to the will of God as I desire. There is a time to plant, and a time to pull up that which is planted, which I could desire might not be yet. But the Lord knoweth what is best, and his will be done. But I will write no more. Hoping to see thee tomorrow, my best affections being commended to yourself, (and) the rest of our friends at Newton, I commit thee to God.

> Your loving wife,
> Margaret Winthrop.
> Sad Boston, 1637

For Mrs. Winthrop at Boston.

Dear [torn],—I am still detained from thee, but it is by the Lord, who hath a greater interest in me than thyself. When his work is done he will restore me to thee again to our mutual comfort: Amen. I thank thee for the sweet Letter: my heart was with thee to have written to thee every day, but business would not permit me. I suppose thou hearest much news from hence: it may be, some grievous to thee: but be not troubled, I assure thee things go well, & they must needs do so, for God is with us & thou shalt see a happy issue. I hope to be with thee to-morrow & a friend or 2, I suppose. So I kiss my sweet wife & rest

Thine Jo: Winthrop
This 6: day
[Reuther and Keller, pp. 163-165]

"My dear children"

Anne Bradstreet (c.1612-1672) is considered by many scholars to be America's first poet. In 1628 the former Anne Dudley married her father's protégé, Simon Bradstreet, and they sailed from England to America two years later. They were among the first white inhabitants of Massachusetts Bay.

Initially the teenaged Anne found it difficult to cope with the crude conditions of pioneer life and began to have doubts about her faith. Because of her husband's prominent position in the colony, however (he was an assistant and then twice governor), she felt compelled to keep her struggles to herself. During those early years she wrote poetry to work through her trials and in that creative exercise found her faith restored and her sanity intact.

In 1650 her brother-in-law, the Rev. John Woodbridge, took her poetry with him to London where he had it published without Anne's knowledge. The Tenth Muse Lately Sprung Up in America made her America's first published poet.

Mrs. Bradstreet wrote not only poetry, but also letters of instruction to her children to encourage them along a godly path. Although the date of this frank letter to her offspring is not known for certain, its intention is clear: to demonstrate the goodness of God in her life and to give them a clear vision of life in Christ to carry them for the rest of their lives.

"Among all my experiences of God's gracious dealings with me, I have constantly observed this, that He hath never suffered me long to sit loose from Him . . ."

My dear children,

I, knowing by experience that the exhortations of parents take most effect when the speakers leave to speak, and those especially sink deepest which are spoke latest, and being ignorant whether on my death bed I shall have opportunity to speak to any of you, much less to all, thought it the best, whilst I was able, to compose some short matters (for what else to call them I know not) and bequeath to you, that when I am no more with you, yet I may be daily in your remembrance (although that is the least in my aim in what I now do), but that you may gain some spiritual advantage by my experience. I have not studied in this you read to show my skill, but to declare the truth, not to set forth myself, but the glory of God. If I had minded the former, it had been perhaps better pleasing to you, but seeing the last is the best, let it be best pleasing to you.

The method I will observe shall be this: I will begin with God's dealing with me from my childhood to this day.

In my young years, about 6 or 7, as I take it, I began to make conscience of my ways, and what I knew was sinful, as lying, disobedience to parents, etc., I avoided it. If at any time I was overtaken with the like evils, it was as a great trouble, and I could not be at rest till by prayer I had confessed it unto God. I was also troubled at the neglect of private duties though too often tardy that way. I also found much comfort in reading the Scriptures, especially those places I thought most concerned my condition, and as I grew to have more understanding, so the more solace I took in them.

In a long fit of sickness which I had on my bed I often communed with my heart and made my supplication to the most High who set me free from that affliction.

But as I grew up to be about 14 or 15, I found my heart more carnal, and sitting loose from God, vanity and the follies of youth take hold of me.

About 16, the Lord laid His hand sore upon me and smote me with the smallpox. When I was in my affliction, I besought the Lord and confessed my pride and vanity, and He was entreated of me and again restored me. But I rendered not to Him according to the benefit received.

After a short time I fell into a lingering sickness like a consumption together with a lameness, which correction I saw the Lord sent to humble and try me and do me good, and it was not altogether ineffectual.

It pleased God to keep me a long time without a child, which was a great grief to me and cost me many prayers and tears before I obtained one, and after him gave me many more of whom I now take the care, that as I have brought you into the world, and with great pains, weakness, cares, and fears brought you to this, I now travail in birth again of you till Christ be formed in you.

Among all my experiences of God's gracious dealings with me, I have constantly observed this, that He hath never suffered me long to sit loose from Him, but by one affliction or other hath made me look home, and search what was amiss; so usually thus it hath been with me that I have no sooner felt my heart out of order, but I have expected correction for it, which most commonly hath been upon my own person in sickness, weakness, pains, sometimes on my soul, in doubts and fears of God's displeasure and my sincerity towards Him; sometimes He hath smote a child with a sickness, sometimes chastened by losses in estate, and these times (through His great mercy) have been the times of my greatest getting and advantage; yea, I have found them the times when the Lord hath manifested the most love to me. Then have I gone to searching and have said with David, "Lord, search me and try me, see what ways of wickedness are in me, and lead me in the way everlasting," and seldom or never but I have found either some sin I lay under which God would have reformed, or some duty neglected which He would have performed, and by His help I have laid vows and bonds upon my soul to perform His righteous commands.

If at any time you are chastened of God, take it as thankfully and joyfully as in greatest mercies, for if ye be His, ye shall reap the greatest benefit by it. It hath been no small support to me in times of darkness when the Almighty hath hid His face from me that yet I have had abundance of sweetness and refreshment after affliction and more circumspection in my walking after I have been afflicted. I have been with God like an untoward child, that no longer than the rod has been on my back (or at least in sight) but I have been apt to forget Him and myself, too. Before I was afflicted, I went astray, but now I keep Thy statutes.

I have had great experience of God's hearing my prayers and returning comfortable answers to me, either in granting the thing I prayed for, or else in satisfying my mind without it, and I have been confident it hath been from Him, because I have found my heart through His goodness enlarged in thankfulness to Him.

I have often been perplexed that I have not found that constant joy in my pilgrimage and refreshing which I supposed most of the servants of God have, although He hath not left me altogether without the witness of His holy spirit, who hath oft given me His word and set to His seal that it shall be well with me. I have sometimes tasted of that hidden manna that the world knows not, and have set up my Ebenezer, and have resolved with myself that against such a promise, such tastes of sweetness, the gates of hell shall never prevail; yet I have many times sinkings and droopings, and not enjoyed that felicity that sometimes I have done. But when I have been in darkness and seen no light, yet have I desired to stay myself upon the Lord, and when I have been in sickness and pain, I have thought if the Lord would but lift up the light of His countenance upon me, although He ground me to powder, it would be but light to me; yea, oft have I thought were I in hell itself and could there find the love of God toward me, it would be a heaven. And could I have been in heaven without the love of God, it would have been a hell to me, for in truth it is the absence and presence of God that makes heaven or hell.

Many times hath Satan troubled me concerning the verity of the Scriptures, many times by atheism how I could know whether there was a God; I never saw any miracles to confirm me, and those which I read of, how did I know but they were feigned? That there is a God my reason would soon tell me by the wondrous works that I see, the vast frame of the heaven and the earth, the order of all things, night and day, summer and winter, spring and autumn, the daily providing for this great household upon the earth, the preserving and directing of all to its proper end. The consideration of these things would with amazement certainly resolve me that there is an Eternal Being. But how should I know He is such a God as I worship in Trinity, and such a Savior as I rely upon? Though this hath thousands of times been suggested to me, yet God hath helped me over. I have argued thus with myself. That there is a God, I see. If ever this God hath revealed himself, it must be in His word, and this must be it or none. Have I not found that operation by it that no human invention can work upon the soul, hath not judgments befallen divers who have scorned and contemned it, hath it not been preserved through all ages maugre all the heathen tyrants and all of the enemies who have opposed it? Is there any story but that which shows the beginnings of times, and how the world came to be as we see? Do we not know the prophecies in it fulfilled which could not have been so long foretold by any but God Himself?

When I have got over this block, then have I another put in my way, that admit this be the true God whom we worship, and that be His word, yet why may not the Popish religion be the right? They have the same God, the same Christ, the same word. They only interpret it one way, we another.

This hath sometimes stuck with me, and more it would, but the vain fooleries that are in their religion together with their lying miracles and cruel persecutions of the saints, which admit were they as they term them, yet not so to be dealt withal.

The consideration of these things and many the like would soon turn me to my own religion again.

But some new troubles I have had since the world has been filled with blasphemy and sectaries, and some who have been accounted sincere Christians have been carried away with them, that sometimes I have said, "Is there faith upon the earth?" and I have not known what to think; but then I have remembered the words of Christ that so it must be, and if it were possible, the very elect should be deceived. "Behold," saith our Savior, "I have told you before." That hath stayed my heart, and I can now say, "Return, O my soul, to the rest, upon this rock Christ Jesus will I build my faith, and if I perish, I perish"; but I know all the Powers of Hell shall never prevail against it. I know whom I have trusted, and whom I have believed, and that He is able to keep that I have committed to His charge.

Now to the King, immortal, eternal and invisible, the only wise God, be honor, and glory for ever and ever, Amen.

This was written in much sickness and weakness, and is very weakly and imperfectly done, but if you can pick any benefit out of it, it is the mark which I aimed at.

[Baym, pp. 136-139]

"My dearly Beloved Friend M.F."

William Penn (1644-1718) believed deeply in the right of each human being to practice his or her religious beliefs, free of government compulsion or censure. A young Englishman during the initial years of Quakerism, he was attracted to the sect's objection to State-sponsored churches, war and oaths. Due to debts owed by the Crown to William's father, Sir William Penn, the young man received a proprietorship of land north of Maryland by King Charles II in 1681. Penn gathered a group of fellow Quakers around him to try a "holy experiment" in which each person would be free to follow his or her own faith in God, no matter the denomination. Pennsylvania, named for Penn's father, also became a model for friendly relations between the white colonists and the Native Americans.

It is no coincidence that the Quakers also were known as the Society of Friends, for they advocated warm, brotherly love and concern toward all people. In the years just before coming to America, Penn wrote to Margaret Fox, the wife of Quakerism's founder George Fox, bringing her up to date on all his family and fellowship's news. It is an obvious demonstration of the special bond that friends in Christ share.

His spelling, punctuation, and capitalization are very much a product of his time—in other words, the king's English!

"o that we may forever be kept in the sweet
& tender powr of the lord, for there is
[no] preservation out of it . . ."

(8 January 1678)

My dearly Beloved Friend M.F.

In dear & everlasting kindness, I do Salute & embrace thee, acknowledging thy great love & regard to me, which hath often refresht my soule in the remembrance of it. & blessed be the pure god of all heavenly riches & goodness that hath given me a name among the liveing, & a place in (the) hearts of his righteous & honorable ones: & truly sweet & precious is the holy fellowship that our dear lord hath given us together in his own pure eternall Spirit, that hath quickened us, & made us neer & very dear, above the life, spirit & friendship of this Corrupt world. o that we may forever be kept in the sweet & tender powr of the lord; for there is [no] preservation out of it, & that this day will (declare), & hath declared already. Truly it is a time of exercise in many respects, but all workes together for good to those that are sinceer, & have their eye to the Lord: verely, the . . . chaff shall be seperated from the wheat; & all these things are for cleansing & brightening the faithfull more & more; that the pure Seed may raign above & over all its oppressors. I shall forbear Perticulers, referring thee to thy dr. daughter, who has had a reall service both in this & other nations. thy dr: & hond husband is well, & in the Service of the great God & King, whos Angell & speciall messenger he is, & woe to them, that rise up agst him in his Lords Service. In generall, the Powr springs & raignes righteous, & will plague the ungodly & unstable that leave their integrity.

My dear wife was well yesterday & my son, a large & active child, my wife is bigg, & expects to lye in the first week in the first month, lett her condition be remembered by thee. Thy son and daughter Rous & their children were well the other day; I have been lately very ill, opprest in body & spirit, but blessed be the god of my life I am finely recover'd. o we are bound up together in everlasting love, precious & Sweet is our heavenly kindred & relation; o how neer & dear are we to one another; o the Powr makes weigh, we cannot forgett one an other, noe time Can wait out, noe distance separate, noe waters quench our love & union, our dear & tender regard to each other. o this is my life, my Joy, & my Crown; it excells the wisdom & glory of the world; yea Prophesy shall cease & miracles shall Cease, but this more excellent way shall endure for ever. I Could not lett thy daughter goe without this short testemony of my love, & due regard to thee, & thy remembrance of me in thy two last letters, very dear to me; as I hope they will always be. salute me dearly to thy dear Son Lowr & daughter, & Daughter Sarah, Sus: & Rachell, & the lord god all mighty have you all ever in his Protection. I am in endless bonds of heavenly friendship, & fellowship.

> Thy endeared
> friend & faithfull
> Brother
> Wm Penn
> [Dunn and Dunn, pp. 518-519]

2

The Battle for Independence:
Letters of the Revolutionary Period

"I feel no great anxiety at the large armyment designed against us. The remarkable interpositions of Heaven in our favour cannot be too gratefully acknowledged."
—Abigail Adams

OVER THE YEARS, the rugged settlements carved out of the American wilderness eventually became cities, with significant populations and healthy economies. A new nation was emerging, one that was too big to remain a simple colony ruled by a monarch across the ocean. The letters that follow give some insight into the personal lives of these early patriots.

"We are spirits"

Benjamin Franklin is one of the best-loved figures in American history. The great patriot and entrepreneur also had a caring nature that came through in his letters of comfort and consolation. Although he was not an evangelical Christian, Franklin professed an active faith in God and the reality of heaven that he drew upon at times of loss. He wrote this letter to soothe his niece with thoughts about the hereafter when his brother John, her stepfather, died. (Miss Hubbard's mother was John Franklin's second wife.)

"A man is not completely born until he is dead. Why then should we grieve, that a new child is born among the immortals, a new member added to their happy society?"

February 23, 1756

Dear Miss Hubbard:

I condole with you. We have lost a most dear and valuable relation. But it is the will of God and nature, that these mortal bodies be laid aside, when the soul is to enter into real life. This is rather an embryo state, a preparation for living.

A man is not completely born until he is dead. Why then should we grieve, that a new child is born among the immortals, a new member added to their happy society? We are spirits. That bodies should be lent us, while they can afford us pleasure, assist us in acquiring knowledge, or in doing good to our fellow creatures, is a kind and benevolent act of God. When they become unfit for these purposes, and afford us pain instead of pleasure, instead of an aid become an encumbrance, and answer none of the intentions for which they were given, it is equally kind and benevolent, that a way is provided by which we may get rid of them. Death is that way. We ourselves, in some cases, prudently choose a partial death. A mangled painful limb, which cannot be restored, we willingly cut off. He who plucks out a tooth, parts with it freely, since the pain goes with it; and he, who quits the whole body, parts at once with all pains and possibilities of pains and diseases which it was liable to, or capable of making him suffer.

Our friend and we were invited abroad on a party of pleasure, which is to last for ever. His chair was ready first, and he is gone before us. We could not all conveniently start together; and why should you and I be grieved at this, since we are soon to follow, and know where to find him?

Adieu,
B. Franklin

[Schuster, pp. 163-164]

The Spiritual Struggle of Sarah Sinons

Sarah Sinons was a young Narragansett Indian who attended a white mission school under Eleazar Wheelock's direction in Lebanon, Connecticut. While it isn't known to whom she wrote this in 1769, what does come through clearly is her sense of struggle in trying to understand, and become, a Christian.

". . . it seems to me all the true Christan never meats with Such a Struggle with Saton as I do and So that maks me fear that I am no Christan becase the Devil is So bese with me more than he is with any one Els. "

I have been this Some time back thinking upon things of Religion; and I think thay do not look So plain to me as I have Seen them and I have a great many weicked thoughts and I donot know what I Shall do if I donot ask Sombodys advise about it for I feel very bad about it; I have thought a quite while that I would Come and talk with the Dr but then I thought again that it will not do me any good; for I have talked with the Dr grant many times and if I do not mind them words that had been already Said to me I Shall have the more to answer for; So I thought I would not go no where to here any thing or no ask any qu-ns about any but I fear it is the works of Saton; and I have mind it till I am undone for Ever and I believe that Satan is besser with me than anybody els in this world Even when I go to Read he taks all my thoughts away upon Somthing Els and many temptations he had before me I thought I never would not till any body of it but as I was at home this after noon all alone I was thinking about thise things and wondering what I Should do. and I thought of a book I had Read onse that when any one was at lost about any thing they must go to there minster and inquire of them and these will lead you into it, and then I think it is my duty to Come and take your advise, and I what want to know is this am I uncurenble or not; the devil is jest Redy Sometimes to make me think that becase I have made a perfertion and do alwas keep upright. and it seems to me all the true Christan never meats with Such a Struggle with Saton as I do and So that maks me fear that I am no Christan becase the Devil is So bese with me more than he is with any one Els. for when I go to try to pray he till me that it will not do any good nither will it merat any thing so he trys Every thing to put me back and o what Shall I do it Seam to me I Could writ all this night to you if it would do any good but I fear it will not. So I Desire to Subscrib my Silfe your most humble and Ever Dutyfull Searvent Sarah Sinons.

[McCallum]

The Nation's First Black Female Author

Phillis Wheatley (c.1754-1784), a slave purchased to be a companion for a tailor's wife in Boston, arrived in the American colonies at about the age of seven. In spite of her bondage, the girl obtained a much better education than most white females of that era after John and Susannah Wheatley discovered her intellectual abilities.

By thirteen Phillis could read Latin, as well as English, and she began to write poetry. "On Messrs. Hussey and Coffin," the first literary work published by a black female in America, appeared publicly in 1770. That same year "On the Death of the Rev. George Whitefield" made the young woman famous.

The Countess of Huntingdon sent for her in 1773, and Phillis once again crossed the Atlantic Ocean, but under far more favorable conditions than the first time. After her London sojourn, she carried on an interesting correspondence with several people on both sides of the Atlantic who involved themselves in her intellectual and spiritual development.

In addition to her intellectual proficiency, Phillis also learned to develop her spirituality as a young woman. Her owners, John and Susannah Wheatley, recognized that the educational training they provided for the girl would be to little avail in the long run were it not reinforced by a sound faith in Jesus Christ.

On May 19, 1772 Miss Wheatley expressed the depths of her love for Christ and her gratitude toward Him in a letter to her sister in Christ, Arbour Tanner, of Newport, Rhode Island, a black servant. More of her letters to Miss Tanner have survived than to any other person.

*"Inexpressibly happy Should we be could
we have a due Sense of the Beauties and
excellence of the Crucified Saviour."*

Boston, May 19, 1772

Dear Sister,

I rec'd your favour of February 6th for which I give you my sincere thanks, I greatly rejoice with you in that realizing view, and I hope experience, of the Saving change which you So emphatically describe. Happy were it for us if we could arrive to that evangelical Repentance, and the true holiness of heart which you mention. Inexpressibly happy Should we be could we have a due Sense of the Beauties and excellence of the Crucified Saviour. In his Crucifixion may be seen marvellous displays of Grace and Love, Sufficient to draw and invite us to the rich and endless treasures of his mercy, let us rejoice in and adore the wonders of God's infinite Love in bringing us from a land Semblant of darkness itself, and where the divine light of revelation (being obscur'd) is as darkness. here, the knowledge of the true God and eternal life are made manifest; But there, profound ignorance overshadows the Land, Your observation is true, namely, that there was nothing in us to recommend us to God. Many of our fellow creatures are pass'd by, when the bowels of divine love expanded towards us. May this goodness & long Suffering of God lead us to unfeign'd repentance. . . .

Til we meet in the regions of consummate bless-edness, let us endeavor by the assistance of divine grace, to live the life, and we Shall die the death of the Righteous. May this be our happy case and of those who are travelling to the region of Felicity is the earnest request of your affectionate

> Friend and hum. Sert.
> Phillis Wheatley
> [Baym, pp. 380-381]

A Lover of Scripture

A London merchant and socially minded Christian named John Thornton had encouraged Phillis to elevate the Bible above all the other books she read so eagerly. This was her response.

> Boston, April 21, 1772

Hon'd, Sir

I rec'd your instructive fav [letter] of Feb. 29, for which, return you ten thousand thanks, I did not flatter myself with the tho'ts of your honouring me with an Answer to my letter, I thank you for recom-mending the Bible to be my chief Study, I find and Acknowledge it the best of Books, it contains an endless treasure of wisdom, and knowledge. O that my eyes were more open'd to see the real worth, and true excellence of the word of truth, my flinty heart Soffen'd with the grateful dews of divine grace and the Stubborn will, and affections, bent on God alone their proper object, and the vitiated palate may be corrected to relish heav'nly things. It has pleas'd God to lay me on a bed of Sickness, and I knew not but my deathbed, but he has been graciously pleas'd to restore me in a great measure. I beg your prayers, that I may be made thankful for his paternal corrections, and that I may make a proper use of them to the glory of his grace. I am Still very weak & the Physicians, seem to think there is danger of consumption. And O that when my flesh and my heart fail me God would be my strength and portion for ever. that I might put my whole trust and Confidence in him, who has promis'd never to forsake those who Seek him with the whole heart. You could not, I am sure have express greater tenderness and affection for me, than by being a welwisher to my Soul, the friends of Souls bear Some resemblance to the father of Spirits and are made partakers of his divine Nature.

I am afraid I have entruded on your patient, but if I had not tho't it ungrateful to omit writing in answer to your favour Should not have troubl'd you, but I can't expect you to answer this,

> I am Sir with greatest respect,
> your very hum. sert.
> Phillis Wheatley

[Baym, p. 380]

44

The Battle for Independence

"On the brink of that Bottomless Profound"

Phillis went to London in the spring with her owner's son at the request of the Countess of Huntingdon, who was quite taken with the black girl's literary talent. During Wheatley's stay in London, Poems on Various Subjects, Religious and Moral *was published there to an enthusiastic reception. She left that place abruptly, however, in the late summer upon learning that her mistress, Susannah Wheatley, had taken ill.*

The young woman wrote this letter to her spiritual benefactor, London merchant John Thornton, on December 1, 1773, not long before the death of her mistress. Its content indicates that the blessed rest of Christians was much on her mind at that time.

Boston, December 1, 1773

Hon'd Sir,

It is with great satisfaction, I acquaint you with my experience of the goodness of God in safely conducting my passage over the might waters, and returning me in safety to my American Friends. I presume you will Join with them and m[e] in praise to God for so distinguishing a favour, it was amazing Mercy, altogether unmerited by me: and if possible it is augmented by the consideration of the bitter r[e]verse, which is the deserved wages of my evil doings. The Apostle Paul, tells us that the wages of Sin is death. I don't imagine he excepted any sin whatsoever being equally hateful in its nature in the sight of God, who is essential Purity.

Should we not sink hon'd Sir, under this Sentence of Death, pronounced on every Sin, from the comparatively least to the greatest, were not this blessed Con[n]trast annexed to it, "But the Gift of God is eternal Life,["] through Jesus Christ our Lord? It is his Gift. O let us be thankful for it! What a load is taken from the Sinner's Shoulder when he thinks that Jesus has done that work for him which he could never have done, and Suffer'd, that punishment of his imputed Rebellions, for which a long Eternity of Torments could not have made sufficient expiation. O that I could meditate continually on this work of wonde[r] in Deity itself. This, which Kings & Prophets have desir'd to see, & have not See[n]. This, which Angels are continually exploring, yet are not equal to the search,—Millions of Ages shall roll away, and they may try in vain to find out to perfection, the sublime mysteries of Christ's Incarnation. Nor will this desir[e] to look into the deep things of God, cease, in the Breasts of glorified Saints & Angels. It's duration will be coeval with Eternity. This Eternity how dreadf[ul,] how delightful! Delightful to those who have an interest in the Crucifi[ed] Saviour, who has dignified our Nature, by seating it at the Right Hand of the divine Majesty.—They alone who are thus interested have Cause to rejoi[ce] even on the brink of that Bottomless Profound: and I doubt not (without the [lea]st Adulation) that you are one of that happy number. O pray that I may be one also, who Shall Join with you in Songs of praise at the Throne of him, who is no respecter of Persons: being equally the great Maker of all:—Therefor disdain not to be called the Father of Humble Africans and Indians; though despised on earth on account of our colour, we have this Consolation, if he enables us to deserve it. "That God dwells in the humble & contrite heart." O that I were more & more possess'd of this inestimable blessing; to be directed by the immediate influence of the divine Spirit in my daily walk & Conversation. . . .

> I am Hon'd Sir
> most respectfully your
> Humble Servt.
> Phillis Wheatley
>
> [Baym, pp. 381-382]

"God grant Deliverance in his own Way and Time"

Although officially a bondwoman, Phillis' owners were part of an "enlightened" social group of Christians who asserted that slavery was incompatible with Christianity. They took pains to nurture Phillis' intelligence as well as her relationship with Christ, taking joy in her fame as a poet that spread beyond America to England.

Susannah Wheatley died in 1774, and Phillis found herself a free woman. Four years later she married another freedman, John Peters, who ended up being imprisoned for debt. Although Phillis died in poverty, and two children preceded her in death, she left behind a joyful legacy of poetry about liberty and justice, as well as freedom in Christ.

A champion of independence and abolition, she launched the black literary movement, as well as black women's literary traditions in America. To the Rev. Samson Oscom, a Mohegan Indian and ordained Presbyterian minister from New London, Connecticut, Phillis

Wheatley described in soaring terms her thoughts about living free.

February 11, 1774

Rev'd and honor'd Sir,

I have this Day received your obliging kind Epistle, and am greatly satisfied with your Reasons respecting Negroes, and think highly reasonable what you offer in Vindication of their natural Rights: Those that invade them cannot be insensible that the divine Light is chasing away the thick Darkness which broods over the Land of Africa; and the Chaos which had reign'd so long, is converting into beautiful Order, and [r]eveals more and more clearly, the glorious Dispensation of civil and religious Liberty, which are so inseparably united, that there is little or no Enjoyment of one without the other: Otherwise, perhaps, the Israelites had been less solicitous for their Freedom from Egyptian slavery; I do not say they would have been contented without it, but no means, for in every human Breast, God has implanted a Principle, which we call Love of Freedom; it is impatient of Oppression, and pants for Deliverance; and by the Leave of our modern Egyptians I will assert, that the same Principle lives in us. God grant Deliverance in his own Way and Time, and get him honour upon all those whose Avarice impels them to countenance and help forward the Calamities of their fellow Creatures. This I desire not for their Hurt, but to convince them of the strange Absurdity of their Conduct whose Words and Actions are so diametrically opposite. How well the Cry for Liberty, and the reverse Disposition for the exercise of oppressive Power over others agree,—I humbly think it does not require the Penetration of a philosopher to determine.—

[Baym, pp. 382-383]

Letters of a Founding Mother

Abigail Smith Adams was an ardent patriot who endured long absences from her husband during the American Revolution. Born in Weymouth, Massachusetts in 1744, she hailed from a distinguished family that had resided in the colonies for five generations at the time of her birth. Although she had no formal education, her keen mind embraced the works of Milton and Shakespeare, Pope and Thomson. She also became fluent in French.

Abigail married John Adams, a lawyer and Harvard graduate, in 1764, and her new spouse further developed her skills in the areas of farming, law, politics and religion. From 1774-1784 the couple was apart more than together due to John's political activities in Philadelphia and abroad. They kept up with each other through a lively, touching correspondence. [Janney, pp. 9-10]

In the following letters to her husband, Abigail Adams expresses her own deeply felt convictions about the establishment of the United States of America.

"In the new Code of Laws which I suppose it will be necessary for you to make I desire you would Remember the Ladies, and be more generous and favourable to them than your ancestors."

November 12, 1775

I could not join to day in the petitions of our worthy parson, for a reconciliation between our, no longer parent State, but tyrant State, and these Colonies.—Let us separate, they are unworthy to be our Breathren. Let us renounce them and instead of supplications as formorly for their prosperity and happiness, Let us beseach the almighty to blast their counsels and bring to Nought all their devices.

June 17, 1776

I feel no great anxiety at the large armyment designed against us. The remarkable interpositions of Heaven in our favour cannot be too gratefully acknowledged. He who fed the Israelites in the wilderness, who cloaths the lilies of the Field and feeds the young Ravens when they cry, will not forsake a people engaged in so righteous cause if we remember his Loving kindness.

March 31, 1776

I long to hear that you have declared an independency—and by the way in the new Code of Laws which I suppose it will be necessary for you to make I desire you would Remember the Ladies, and be more generous and favourable to them than your ancestors. Do not put such unlimited power into the hands of the Husbands. Remember all Men would be tyrants if they could. If perticuliar care and attention is not paid to the Ladies we are determined to foment a Rebelion, and will not hold ourselves bound by any Laws in which we have no voice, or Representation.

That your Sex are Naturally Tyrannical is a Truth so thoroughly established as to admit of no dispute, but such of you as wish to be happy willingly, give us the harsh title of Master for the more tender and endearing one of Friend. Men of Sense in all Ages abhor those customs which treat us only as the vassals of your Sex. Regard us then as Beings placed by providence under your protection and in imitation of the Supreem Being make use of that power only for our happiness.

July 21, 1776

Last Thursday after hearing a very Good Sermon I went with the Multitude into Kings Street to hear the proclamation for independence read and proclaimed. Some Field pieces with the Train were brought there, the troops appeard under Arms and all the inhabitants assembled there. The cry from the Belcona, was God Save our American States and then 3 cheers rended the air, the Bells rang, the privateers fired, the forts and Batteries, the cannon were discharged, the platoons followed and every face appeared joyfull. After dinner the kings arms were taken down from the State House and every vestage of him from every place in which it appeard and burnt in King Street. Thus ends royall Authority in this State, and all the people shall say Amen.

[Reuther and Keller, pp. 391-393]

"You are accountable to your Master"

Uniquely positioned in American history as the wife of one President and the mother of another, Abigail Adams was a prodigious letter writer in her day. She had to be in order to keep up with her husband, John, who traveled widely from 1774-1784 helping to forge America's nationhood. However, Abigail also frequently wrote to her children as they grew up and started pursuing their own interests and goals. While she strongly encouraged their intellectual development, she insisted that above all, they must establish a relationship with the Almighty and live according to His principles. Only then would they be people of character, and their lives truly worthwhile. In this letter, written to her son John Quincy in the winter of 1779-80, she made her conviction uncompromisingly clear.

My Dear John:

Improve your understanding for acquiring useful knowledge and virtue, such as will render you an ornament to society, an Honour to your Country and a Blessing to your parents. Great Learning and superior abilities, should you ever possess them, will be of little value and small Estimation, unless Virtue, Honour, Truth and integrity are added to them. Adhere to those religious Sentiments and principals which are early instilled into your mind and remember that you are accountable to your Maker for all your words and actions. Let me injoin it upon you to attend constantly and steadfastly to the precepts and instructions of your Father as you value the happiness of your Mother and your own welfare. . . .

The Battle for Independence

I had much rather you should have found your Grave in the ocean you have cross[e]d or any untimely death crop you in your Infant years, rather than see you an immoral profligate or a Graceless child.

[Levin, pp. 119-120]

"We must not stray from the Writ of right"

*On December 16, 1773 the Boston Tea Party sig-
naled the beginning of a transition. Americans went
from being locally oriented, British-dominated colonists
to national revolutionaries. In the thick of the patriot's
battle against tyranny stood John Adams (1735-1826),
a Harvard-educated lawyer. From 1774 to 1777 he
represented Massachusetts at the First and Second Continental Congresses. In January, 1776 he received a letter from Virginia lawyer George Wythe requesting that
Adams design a constitutional government that would
prepare the American colonists for war against Britain.
Adams's brief response attests to his strong conviction
that the cornerstone of any new government needed to be
the Christian faith with its principles.*

*"The foundation of every nation is some principle or
passion in the minds of the people."*

Dear Mr. Wythe,

The foundation of every nation is some principle
or passion in the minds of the people. The noblest
principles and most generous affections in our
Christian character, then, have the fairest chance to
support the noblest and the most generous models
of civil covenant. If liberty and justice for all men is

to be ensured then we cannot, we dare not we must not stray from the Writ of right.

[Grant, p. 115]

From the First U.S. Commander in Chief

George Washington (1732-1799) spent his early adulthood with the Virginia militia, serving mainly in the French and Indian Wars. In 1755 he took charge of all Virginia forces; however, he retired from military pursuits in 1759 to serve as a member of Virginia's House of Burgesses. A prosperous gentleman farmer, Washington risked his life, livelihood and considerable possessions in 1774 when he joined the patriot cause, taking command of the Virginia militia. He so distinguished himself that the following year the Second Continental Congress made him commander-in-chief of the entire Continental Army.

Following his deft crossing of the Delaware River to defeat the British forces in Trenton, New Jersey on Christmas night, 1776, Washington held the fledgling army together throughout the following year's disappointments. One of the biggest tests for the troops came at Valley Forge's difficult winter encampment.

In this directive to his men General Washington challenged them to rise to the occasion of their circumstances; they had suffered defeat upon defeat on the battlefield and found themselves tired, cold and low on food and clothing. The situation, though not entirely desperate, was severe. Washington's conviction that they would triumph over their circumstances shines through this letter.

"The General directs . . . that the Chaplains perform divine service. . . . And earnestly exhorts, all officers and soldiers, whose absence is not indispensibly necessary, to attend with reverance the solemnities of the day."

Head Quarters, at the Gulph, December 17, 1777. Parole Warwick. Countersigns Woodbridge, Winchester.

The Commander in Chief with the highest satisfaction expressed his thanks to the officers and soldiers for the fortitude and patience with which they have sustained the fatigues of the Campaign. Altho' in some instances we unfortunately failed, yet upon the whole Heaven hath smiled on our Arms and crowned them with signal success; and we may upon the best grounds conclude, that by a spirited continuance of the measures necessary for our defence we shall finally obtain the end of our Warfare, Independence, Liberty and Peace. These are blessings worth contending for at every hazard. But we hazard nothing. The power of America alone, duly exerted, would have nothing to dread from the force of Britain. Yet we stand not wholly upon our ground. France yields us every aid we ask, and there are reasons to believe the period is not very distant, when she will take a more active part, by declaring war against the British Crown. Every motive therefore, irresistibly urges us, nay commands us, to a firm and manly perseverance in our opposition to our cruel oppressors, to slight difficulties, endure hardships, and contemn every danger. The General ardently wishes it were now in his power, to conduct the troops into the best winter quarters. But where are these to be found? Should we retire to the interior parts of the State, we should find them crowded with virtuous citizens, who, sacrificing their all, have left Philadelphia, and fled thither for protection. To their distresses humanity forbids us to add. This is not all, we should leave a vast extent of fertile country to be despoiled and ravaged by the enemy, from which they would draw vast supplies, and where many of our firm friends would be exposed to all the miseries of the most insulting and wanton depredation. A train of evils might be enumerated, but these will suffice. These considerations make it indispensably necessary for the army to take such a position, as will enable it most effectually to prevent distress and to give the most extensive security; and in that position we must make ourselves the best shelter in our power. With activity and diligence Huts may be erected that will be warm and dry. In these the troops will be compact, more secure against surprises than if in a divided state and at hand to protect the country. These cogent reasons have determined the General to take post in the neighborhood of this camp; and influenced by them, he persuades himself, that the officers and soldiers, with one heart, and one mind, will resolve to surmount every difficulty, with a fortitude and patience, becoming their profession, and the sacred cause in which they are engaged. He himself will share in the hardship, and partake of every inconvenience.

Tomorrow being the day set apart by the Honorable Congress for public Thanksgiving and Praise; and duty calling us devoutly to express our grateful acknowledgements to God for the manifold blessings he has granted us. The General directs that the army remain in it's present quarters, and that the Chaplains perform divine service with their several Corps and brigades. And earnestly exhorts, all officers and soldiers, whose absence is not indispensibly necessary, to attend with reverance the solemnities of the day.

[Washington, pp. 280-281]

Washington's Critics

On taking charge of the Continental Army in June, 1775, Washington took a largely ragtag group of local militiamen and turned them into a national fighting force with enough discipline and resolve to defeat the troops of the British Empire, the greatest army in the world. But that happened over many wandering and slow steps that took him from one engagement to the next, including souring defeats and divinely appointed victories, such as the Battle of Brooklyn Heights.

Although George Washington is an icon in American history, "the father of his country," he was not without his critics during the long and winding years of the American Revolution. The following letter to General Thomas Conway, dated c. November 5, 1777, shows us, however, that he had a sense of humor about his detractors.

Sir:

A Letter which I receivd last Night, containd the following paragraph.

In a Letter from Genl. Conway to Genl. Gates he says: "Heaven has been determind to save your Country; or a weak General and bad Councellors would have ruind it."

> I am Sir Yr. Hble Servt.
> Geo. Washington

[Washington, p. 280]

A Patriot's Loyalty

One of the best orators among America's Founding Fathers, Patrick Henry (1736-1799) is best remembered for what he said in 1775 before the Virginia Assembly. He proposed a radical motion that would provide for the arming and training of militiamen in a fight against Great Britain. In that memorable speech he proclaimed, "I do not know what course others may take, but as for me, give me liberty or give me death."

Henry also served as a delegate to the First and Second Continental Congresses in which those present decided the course of the new nation. During the Revolution he became the governor of Virginia, a post that he held from 1776-1779 and again from 1784-1786.

During his first term, the great patriot received an anonymous letter from one of his "Philadelphia friends" warning him of George Washington's incompetence to lead the Continental Army. The message incensed and worried Henry, who quickly wrote to his fellow Virginian to warn Washington of a possible conspiracy against him. When the general failed to respond, Henry once again wrote him to make sure the initial letter had reached Washington. The nation's future was riding on that general's leadership. Henry's second message once again assured Washington of his undying respect and loyalty. The beleaguered general's response follows it.

"I cannot help assuring you, on this occasion, of the high sense of gratitude which all ranks of men, in this native country, bear to you."

Williamsburg,
March 5th, 1778.

Dear Sir,

By an express which Colonel Finnie sent to camp, I enclosed you an anonymous letter, which I hope got safe to hand. I am anxious to hear something that will serve to explain the strange affair, which I am now informed is taken up respecting you. Mr. Custis has just paid us a visit, and by him I learn sundry particulars concerning General Mifflin, that much surprised me. It is very hard to trace the schemes and windings of the enemies to America. I really thought that man its friend: however, I am too far from him to judge of his present temper.

While you face the armed enemies of our liberty in the field, and by the favour of God, have been kept unhurt, I trust your country will never harbour in her bosom the miscreant who would ruin her best supporter. I wish not to flatter; but when arts, unworthy honest men, are used to defame and traduce you, I think it not amiss, but a duty, to assure you of that estimation in which the public hold you. Not that I think any testimony I can bear is necessary for your support, or private satisfaction; for a bare recollection of what is past must give you sufficient pleasure in every circumstance of life. But I cannot help assuring you, on this occasion, of the high sense of gratitude which all ranks of men, in this native country, bear to you. It will give me sincere pleasure to manifest my regards, and render my best services to you or yours. I do not like to make a parade of these things, and I know you are not fond of it: however, I hope the occasion will plead my excuse.

The assembly have, at length, empowered the executive here, to provide the Virginia troops serving with you with clothes, &c. I am making provision accordingly, and hope to do something toward it. Every possible assistance from government is afforded the commissary of provisions, whose department has not been attended to. It was taken up by me too late to do much. Indeed, the load of business devolved on me is too great to be managed well. A French ship mounting thirty guns, that has been long chased by the English cruisers, has got into Carolina, as I hear last night.

Wishing you all possible felicity, I am, my dear sir,

> Your ever affectionate friend,
> And very humble servant,
> P. Henry. [sic]

Valley Forge,
March 27th, 1778.

Dear Sir,

About eight days past, I was honoured with your favour of the 20th ultimo. Your friendship, sir, in transmitting me the anonymous letter you had received, lays me under the most grateful obligations; and, if anything could give a still further claim to my acknowledgements, it is the very polite and delicate terms in which you have been p[ained] to make the communication.

I have ever been happy in supposing that I held a place in your esteem, and the proof of it you have afforded on this occasion makes me peculiarly so. The favourable light in which you hold me is truly flattering; but I should feel much regret if I thought the happiness of America so intimately connected with my personal welfare, as you obligingly seem to consider it. All I can say is, that she has ever had, and I trust she ever will have, my honest exertions to promote her interest. I cannot hope that my services have been the best, but my heart tells me they have been the best that I could render.

That I may have erred in using the means in my power for accomplishing the objects of the arduous, exalted station with which I am honoured, I cannot doubt; nor do I wish my conduct to be exempted from the reprehension it may deserve. Error is the portion of humanity, and to censure it, whether committed by this or that public character, is the prerogative of freemen.

This is not the only secret, insidious attempt that has been made to wound my reputation. There have been others equally base, cruel, and ungenerous; because conducted with as little frankness, and proceeding from views perhaps, as personally interested.

I am, dear sir, &c.
Geo. Washington
[Wirt, pp. 229-232]

To a Future Son-in-Law

Founding Father Samuel Adams (1722-1803) had strong opinions about most subjects, and he rarely hesitated to join or enflame a controversy. Boston-born and Harvard-educated, Adams engaged in the brewery business and served as a tax collector before entering the volatile political arena of the 1760's. He organized resistance to the 1765 Stamp Act and participated in the upheaval that led to the Boston Massacre. Adams also was the primary leader of the Boston Tea Party in 1773 and helped form the Sons of Liberty.

A second cousin to John Adams, Samuel was a delegate to both Continental Congresses and a signer of the Declaration of Independence. While serving in the Continental Congress in 1780, Adams had more than revolution on his mind, though. Life went on within his family as well, and he wrote this fatherly letter to his daughter Hannah's prospective husband, "T. Wells," about the sacredness and responsibilities of marriage.

"Religion in a family is at once its brightest ornament and its best security."

November 22, 1780

Although I have not yet acknowledged the obliging letter you wrote to me some time ago, I would not have you entertain a doubt of my sincere respect and the confidence I place in you. I think I gave you the strongest proof of this when I was last in Boston.

From that moment I have considered myself particularly interested in your welfare. It cannot indeed be otherwise, since I then consented that you should form the most intimate connection with the dear girl whom I pride myself in calling my daughter. I did this with caution and deliberation; and having done it, I am now led to contemplate the relation in which I am myself to stand with you, and I can (hardly) forbear the same style in this letter, which I should take the liberty to use if I was writing to her.

The marriage state was designed to complete the sum of human happiness in this life. It sometimes proves otherwise; but this is owing to the parties themselves, who either rush into it without due consideration, or fail in point of discretion in their conduct towards each other afterwards. It requires judgment on both sides, to conduct with exact propriety; for man, yet as the management of a family in many instances necessarily devolves on the woman, it is difficult always to determine the line between the authority of the one and the subordination of the other. Perhaps the advice of the good bishop of St. Asaph on another occasion, might be adopted on this, and that is, not to govern too much.

When the married couple strictly observe the great rules of honor and justice towards each other, differences, if any happen, between them, must proceed from small and trifling circumstances. Of what consequence is it whether a turkey is brought on the table boiled or roasted? And yet, how often are the passions suffered to interfere in such mighty disputes, till the tempers of both become so soured that they can scarcely look upon each other with any tolerable degree of good humor.

I am not led to this particular mode of treating the subject from an apprehension of more than common danger, that such kind of fracas will frequently take place in that connection, upon which, much of my future comfort in life will depend. I am too well acquainted with the liberality of your way of thinking to harbor such a jealousy; and I think I can trust to my daughter's discretion if she will only promise to exercise it.

I feel myself at this moment so domestically disposed that I could say a thousand things to you, if I had leisure. I could dwell on the importance of piety and religion, of industry and frugality, of prudence, economy, regularity and an even government, all which are essential to the well being of a family. But I have not time. I cannot however help repeating piety, because I think it indispensible. Religion in a family is at once its brightest ornament and its best security. The first point of justice, says a writer I have met with, consists in piety; nothing certainly being so great a debt upon us, as to render to the Creator and Preserver those acknowledgements which are due to Him for our Being, and the hourly protection he affords us.

[Cousins, pp. 353-354]

3

The Young Republic:
Letters of the
Post-Revolutionary Period

DEMOCRACY—GOVERNMENT "OF the people, by the people and for the people"—was considered a radical and risky enterprise in the late eighteenth century. The bloodbath of the French Revolution was proof positive to some that the people could not be trusted to govern themselves. What made the American experiment in representative government succeed where others failed? One identifiable difference was its moral and spiritual foundation. The following letters make it clear that the founding fathers (and mothers) of this fledgling republic, while not all committed believers, shared a deep respect for the morality and ethics of the Christian faith.

In God We Trust

At the end of the War for Independence, George Washington received a number of congratulatory letters from various churches. Throughout his public career he corresponded with many religious bodies, always careful not to favor one Christian expression over another. The letter that follows is typical of those he wrote in the Revolution's aftermath. In it he expresses a deep gratitude to God for the cessation and outcome of the conflict, as well as his conviction that it was a God-ordained and righteous cause whose very purpose was to establish civil and religious liberty.

Historians often assert that Washington clung to deism, the belief that while God created the world, He then stepped back to let humans run things without His help. This letter, among many other evidences throughout Washington's life, proves otherwise.

"Disposed, at every suitable opportunity to acknowledge publicly our infinite obligations to the Supreme Ruler of the Universe for rescuing our Country from the brink of destruction . . ."

To the Minister, Elders, Deacons, and Members of the Reformed German Congregation of New York, November 27, 1783

The illustrious and happy event, the end of the War, on which you are pleased to congratulate and welcome me to this City, demands all our gratitude; while the favorable sentiments you have thought proper to express of my conduct, entitles you to my warmest acknowledgments.

Disposed, at every suitable opportunity to acknowledge publicly our infinite obligations to the Supreme Ruler of the Universe for rescuing our Country from the brink of destruction; I cannot fail at this time to ascribe all the honor of our late successes to the same glorious Being. And if my humble exertions have been made in any degree subservient to the execution of the divine purposes, a contemplation of the benediction of Heaven on our righteous Cause, the approbation of my virtuous Countrymen, and the testimony of my own Conscience, will be a sufficient reward and augment my felicity beyond anything which the world can bestow.

The establishment of Civil and Religious Liberty was the Motive which induced me to the Field; the object is attained, and it now remains to be my earnest wish and prayer, that the Citizens of the United States would make a wise and virtuous use of the blessings, placed before them; and that the reformed German Congregation in New York; may not only be conspicuous for their religious character, but as exemplary, in support of our inestimable acquisitions, as their reverend Minister has been in the attainment of them.

George Washington

[Cousins, pp. 57-58]

A Defender of Religious Freedom

At the time of the Revolution, nine colonies had official churches that gave them a privileged position with the state; they were vested with certain powers denied to other denominations and their members, as well as supported from the public coffers. Founding Father Thomas Jefferson opposed having a state-sanctioned religion that would make it mandatory for its citizens to be members.

In 1777 he drew up a law for Virginia, the Statute of Virginia for Religious Freedom, that was enacted nine years later. It declared his belief that all people should be free to profess their own convictions in religious matters. Jefferson considered it one of his three most important achievements, along with writing the Declaration of Independence and founding the University of Virginia. He maintained that truth was great enough to prevail when left to itself.

His views weren't always popular; many Americans viewed his sometimes unorthodox beliefs with suspicion. He created a "Jefferson Bible" in which he removed all passages from the Scriptures that referred to God's miraculous interventions. When Jefferson won the Presidency in 1800, not a small number of Americans feared the nation's impending moral collapse. He was viewed by many as an enemy of religion, an atheist, an anti-Christ.

Some older women in Massachusetts responded to his election by hiding their Bibles in butter coolers and slipping those into their wells, fearing they'd be confiscated by the government.

Identified by most historians as a deist, Thomas Jefferson actually was an eclectic in his religious convictions. He attended the Anglican Church all his life and served as a vestryman in it. He viewed that fellowship as possessing more style than substance, however, and in his later life came under the influence of the English scientist and Unitarian, Joseph Priestly. Unitarianism taught that all people would be saved, that Jesus was man and not God, and it also rejected the miraculous Virgin Birth.

Whatever Jefferson's shortcomings in religious matters, he maintained a firm attachment to Christianity, as well as to the importance of prayer and personal piety. In the following letter to his nephew, Peter Carr, he expounded on the importance of religious faith.

"The moral sense, or conscience, is as much a part of man as his leg or arm. . . . It may be strengthened by exercise, as may any particular limb of the body."

My Dear Peter,

He who made us would have been a pitiful bungler, if he had made the rules of our moral conduct a matter of science. For one man of science, there are thousands who are not. What would have become of them? Man was destined for society. His morality, therefore, was to be formed to this object. He was endowed with a sense of right and wrong, merely relative to this. . . . The moral sense, or conscience, is as much a part of man as his leg or arm. It is given to all human beings in a stronger or weaker degree, as force of members is given them in a greater or less degree. It may be strengthened by exercise, as may any particular limb of the body. This sense is submitted, indeed, in some degree, to the guidance of reason; but it is a small stock which is required for this; even a less one than what we call common sense.

State a moral case to a plowman and a professor. The former will decide it as well, and often better than the latter, because he had not been led astray by artificial rules. In this branch, therefore, read good books, because they will encourage, as well as direct your feelings. The writings of Sterne, particularly, form the best course of morality that ever was written. Besides these, read the books mentioned in the enclosed paper, and above all things, lose no occasion of exercising your dispositions to be grateful, to be generous, to be charitable, to be humane, to be true, just, firm, orderly, courageous, etc. Consider every act of this kind, as an exercise which will strengthen your moral faculties and increase your worth.

Religion. Your reason is now mature enough to examine this object. In the first place, divest yourself of all bias in favor of novelty and singularity of opinion. Indulge them in any other subject rather than that of religion. It is too important, and the consequences of error may be too serious. On the other hand, shake off all the fears and servile prejudices, under which weak minds are servilely crouched. Fix reason firmly in her seat, and call to her tribunal every fact, every opinion. Question with boldness even the existence of a God; because, if there be one, he must more approve of the homage of reason, than that of blindfolded fear.

You will naturally examine first the religion of your own country. Read the Bible, then, as you would read Livy or Tacitus. The facts which are within the ordinary course of nature, you will believe on the authority of the writer, as you do those of the same kind in Livy and Tacitus. The testimony of the writer weighs in their favor, in one scale, and their not being against the laws of nature, does not weigh against them. But those facts in the Bible which contradict the laws of nature, must be examined with more care, and under a variety of faces. Here you must recur to the pretensions of the writer to inspiration from God. Examine upon what evidence his pretensions are founded, and whether that evidence is so strong, as that its falsehood would be more improbable than a change in the laws of nature, in the case he relates.

[Schuster, p. 793]

Benjamin Franklin's Creed

Few people in American history have accomplished as much as Benjamin Franklin (1706-1790). He was a U.S. diplomat, inventor, physicist, politician and printer, among other things. Included among his impressive exploits are Franklin's founding of the nation's first subscription library, as well as the American Philosophical Society, which he also served as its first president. He also published Poor Richard's Almanack, *invented the lightning rod, served as a delegate to the Continental Congresses, helped draft the Declaration of Independence and invented bifocals.*

During George Whitefield's pre-Revolutionary War revivals in Philadelphia, Franklin provided considerable support, and they remained lifelong friends. However, he could not bring himself to embrace Whitefield's evangelical faith.

In 1790 a great admirer of Franklin wrote to ask his opinion about religion in general and Jesus in particular. Ezra Stiles (1727-1795) served at that time as the president of Yale College. Franklin responded on March 9; he died the following month.

Here is my creed. I believe in one God, Creator of the Universe. That He governs it by His providence. That He ought to be worshiped. That the most acceptable service we render to Him is doing good to His other children. That the soul of man is immortal, and will be treated with justice in another life respecting its conduct in this.

Reverend and Dear Sir,

I received your kind letter of January 28, and am glad you have at length received the portrait of Governor Yale from his family, and deposited it in the college library. He was a great and good man, and had the merit of doing infinite service to your country by his munificence to that institution. The honor you propose doing me by placing mine in the same room with his is much too great for my deserts; but you always had a partiality for me, and to that it must be ascribed. I am however too much obliged to Yale College, the first learned society that took notice of me and adorned me with its honors, to refuse a request that comes from it through so esteemed a friend. But I do not think any one of the portraits you mention, as in my possession, worthy of the place and company you propose to place it in. You have an excellent artist lately arrived. If he will undertake to make one for you, I shall cheerfully pay the expense; but he must not delay setting about it, or I may slip through his fingers, for I am now in my eighty-fifth year, and very infirm.

I send with this a very learned work, as it seems to me, on the ancient Samaritan coins, lately printed in Spain, and at least curious for the beauty of the impression. Please to accept it for your college library. I have subscribed for the Encyclopaedia now printing here, with the intention of presenting it to the college. I shall probably depart before the work is finished, but shall leave directions for its continuance to the end. With this you will receive some of the first numbers.

You desire to know something of my religion. It is the first time I have been questioned upon it. But I cannot take your curiosity amiss, and shall endeavor in a few words to gratify it. Here is my creed. I believe in one God, Creator of the Universe. That He governs it by His providence. That He ought to be worshiped. That the most acceptable service we render to Him is doing good to His other children. That the soul of man is immortal, and will be treated with justice in another life respecting its conduct in this. These I take to be the fundamental principles of all sound religion, and I regard them as you do in whatever sect I meet with them.

As to Jesus of Nazareth, my opinion of whom you particularly desire, I think the system of morals and his religion, as he left them to us, the best the world ever saw or is likely to see; but I apprehend it has received various corrupting changes, and I have with most of the present dissenters in England, some doubts as to his divinity; though it is a question I do not dogmatize upon, having never studied it, and think it needless to busy myself with it now, when I expect soon an opportunity of knowing the truth with less trouble. I see no harm, however, in its being believed, if that belief has the good consequence, as probably it has, of making his doctrines more respected and better observed; especially as I do not perceive, that the Supreme takes its aims, by distinguishing the unbelievers in His government of the world with any peculiar marks of His displeasure.

I shall only add, respecting myself, that, having experienced the goodness of that Being in conducting me prosperously through a long life, I have no doubt of its continuance in the next, though without the smallest conceit of meriting such goodness. My sentiments on this head you will see in the copy of an old letter enclosed, which I wrote in answer to one from a zealous religionist, whom I had relieved in a paralytic case by electricity, and who, being afraid I should grow proud upon it, sent me his serious though rather impertinent caution. I send you also the copy of another letter, which will show something of my disposition relating to religion. With great and sincere esteem and affection, I am, your obliged and old friend and most obedient humble servant,

B. Franklin

P.S. . . . I confide, that you will not expose me to criticism and censure by publishing any part of this communication to you. I have ever let others enjoy their religious sentiments, without reflecting on them for those that appeared to me unsupportable and even absurd. All sects here, and we have a great variety, have experienced my good will in assisting them with subscriptions for building their new places of worship; and, as I have never opposed any of their doctrines, I hope to go out of the world in peace with them all.

[Baym, Nina, pp. 224-225]

Patriot and Lover of God's Word

At twenty-nine, John Jay (1745-1829) became the youngest delegate to the Continental Congress in Philadelphia. He was among the most conservative members of that esteemed gathering, consisting of such fiery men as Samuel Adams and Patrick Henry. At the time of the Revolution Jay served as the State of New York's Chief Justice. Afterward he authored The Federalist Papers, *along with Alexander Hamilton and James Madison.*

When George Washington assembled his first presidential administration, he told Jay to take first choice of the available positions; the forty-four-year-old chose to become the nation's first Chief Justice, a position he held for six years. After going to London at Washington's request to represent U.S. interests there, Jay returned to New York and served as its governor until 1801, when he retired from public life.

Aside from politics, Jay was an ardent Christian who served as a president of the American Bible Society, an organization that his son was instrumental in founding. Throughout his retirement years, Jay remained active in church affairs. The central theme of his faith was the "truth and simplicity of the Gospel" [Cousin, p. 360]. He also believed in the literal truth of the Bible, unlike his compatriots Thomas Jefferson, James Madison and John Adams.

Jay often corresponded about matters of faith and practice with a Congregational minister named Jedidiah Morse, a man whose interests were not confined to theology. He is also known as the father of American geography because of the books he wrote in that field. This excerpt of a letter written to Morse in the winter of 1797 concerns John Jay's view of the Bible.

"I believe the fact to be, that except the Bible there is not a true history in the world."

February 28, 1797

My dear Reverend Morse,

. . . . It is to be regretted, but so I believe the fact to be, that except the Bible there is not a true history in the world. Whatever may be the virtue, discernment, and industry of the writers, I am persuaded that truth and error (though in different degrees) will imperceptibly become and remain mixed and blended until they shall be separated forever by the great and last refining fire.

John Jay

[Cousins, p. 362]

The Final Words of a Man of Honor

Born in the British West Indies in 1755, Alexander
Hamilton (1755-1804) went to King's College (now Co-
lumbia University) in New York at the age of eighteen.
There he amazed his peers and professors by writing impressive political pamphlets in support of the American patriots. When the Revolution commenced, Hamilton so
distinguished himself that George Washington made him
his personal secretary and aide-de-camp.

Following the Revolution, Hamilton served a term in
the Continental Congress, then entered private law
practice in New York City. He, along with James Madison and John Jay, also wrote the distinguished Federalist Papers in support of the new Constitution. In 1789
he became the first Secretary of the Treasury, favoring a
strong central government and helping to establish the
new nation's economic system. In addition, Hamilton
established a national bank and mint, and he worked
aggressively to overcome the national debts left from the
war. He and Thomas Jefferson experienced a strong rift
over clashing political philosophies; Jefferson envisioned
a nation ruled by ordinary people educated in public
schools, basically small farmers who were perfectly capable of ruling themselves. Hamilton, on the other hand,
believed in an America in which a small elite dominated.
Two political parties formed around them, the Demo-
cratic-Republicans and the Federalists respectively.

In 1795 Alexander Hamilton resigned his "cabinet"
post to pursue a private law practice once again. Still active in politics, he served as head of the New York Federalist party. He had enough influence to deny Aaron Burr, a

man he deeply distrusted, the presidency in 1800 and in 1804, the New York governorship. Burr challenged him to a duel, and they faced each other in Weehawken, New Jersey on July 11, 1804. Hamilton loathed dueling, considering it a decadent and archaic method of problem-solving, one that had led to his own son's death in 1801. However, he also believed that his honor demanded both that he accept Burr's challenge—and that he not shoot to kill. The decision to fire into the air led to his death on July 12. He wrote this letter to his wife the night before the "interview" with Burr.

"I shall cherish the sweet hope of meeting you in a better world. Adieu, best of wives—best of women. Embrace all my darling children for me."

July 10, 1804

This letter, my dear Eliza, will not be delivered to you, unless I shall first have terminated my earthly career, to begin, as I humbly hope, from redeeming grace and divine mercy, a happy immortality. If it had been possible for me to have avoided the interview, my love for you and my precious children would have been alone a decisive motive. But it was not possible, without sacrifices which would have rendered me unworthy of you, and exposing you to the anguish I know you would feel. Nor could I dwell on the topic, lest it should unman me. The consolations of religion, my beloved, can alone support you; and these you have a right to enjoy. Fly to the bosom of your God, and be comforted. With my last idea I shall cherish the sweet hope of meeting you in a better world. Adieu, best of wives—best of women. Embrace all my darling children for me.

[Cousins, p. 341]

"I have tasted the bitter cup"

Among the correspondents of patriot, first lady and prolific letter writer Abigail Adams (1744-1818) was the nation's third president, Thomas Jefferson (1743-1826). These two keen and opinionated intellectuals were loathe to hold back when in disagreement with each other, however. A major rift occurred between them when Abigail came to the conclusion that Jefferson, who had served as John Adams' vice-president, was deriding her husband's legacy over some political issue on which they differed—and they differed on many. Adams was a Federalist who believed in a strong central government run by an American upper class, while Jefferson thought that in order for democracy to work, all people needed to be educated, not just a privileged few, and that the ordinary folks should take their part in leading a smaller government.

Jefferson and Mrs. Adams clashed so strongly that they went six years without writing to each other. The event that melted the iciness between them was the death of Jefferson's daughter, Mary Jefferson Eppes, on April 17, 1804. Abigail's mother's heart recalled how, when Mary ventured to be with her father in Paris in 1787, the girl's first European stop was London. Mary was put into Abigail's care until the reunion with her father.

Jefferson maintained a strong and tender affection for his two daughters over the years and corresponded with them prodigiously whenever they were apart. In the children's youth their father admonished them to pray often and write him the long letters to which he so eagerly looked forward. Mary passed away in her late twenties; Jefferson and Abigail Adams were both moved to reestablish their old friendship.

"I have tasted the bitter cup, and bow with reverence, and humility before the great dispenser of it, without whose permission, and over ruling providence, not a sparrow falls to the ground."

Quincy May 20th 1804

Sir

Had you been no other than the private inhabitant of Monticello, I should e'er this time have addrest you, with that sympathy, which a recent event had awakend in my Bosom. But reasons of various kinds withheld my pen, until the powerfull feelings of my heart, have burst through the restraint, and called upon me to shed the tear of sorrow over the departed remains, of your beloved and deserving daughter, an event which I most sincerely mourn.

The attachment which I formed for her, when you committed her to my care: upon her arrival in a foreign Land: has remained with me to this hour, and the recent account of her death, which I read in a late paper, brought fresh to my remembrance the strong sensibility she discoverd, tho but a child of nine years of age at having been seperated from her Friends, and country, and brought, as she expressed it, "to a strange land amongst strangers." The tender scene of her seperation from me, rose to my recollection, when she clung around my neck and wet my Bosom with her tears, saying, "O! now I have learnt to Love you, why will they tear me from you."

It has been some time since that I conceived of any event in this Life, which could call forth, feelings of mutual sympathy. But I know how closely entwined around a parents heart, are those chords which bind the filial to the parental Bosom, and when snaped assunder, how agonizing the pangs of seperation.

I have tasted the bitter cup, and bow with reverence, and humility before the great dispenser of it, without whose permission, and over ruling providence, not a sparrow falls to the ground. That you may derive comfort and consolation in this day of your sorrow and affliction, from that only source calculated to heal the wounded heart—a firm belief in the Being: perfections and attributes of God, is the sincere and ardent wish of her, who once took pleasure in subscribing Herself your Friend

Washington June 13.04.

Dear Madam

The affectionate sentiments which you have had the goodness to express in your letter of May 20. towards my dear departed daughter, have awakened in me sensibilities natural to the occasion, and recalled your kindnesses to her which I shall ever remember with gratitude and friendship. I can assure you with truth they had made an indelible impression on her mind, and that, to the last, on our meetings after long separations, whether I had heard lately of you, and how you did, were among the earliest of her enquiries.

In giving you this assurance I perform a sacred duty for her, and at the same time am thankful for the occasion furnished me of expressing my regret that circumstances should have arisen which have seemed to draw a line of separation between us. The friendship with which you honoured me has ever been valued, and fully reciprocated; and altho' events have been passing which might be trying to some minds, I never believed yours to be of that kind, nor felt that my own was. Neither my estimate of your character, nor the esteem founded in that, have ever been lessened for a single moment, although doubts whether it would be acceptable may have forbidden manifestations of it. Mr. Adams's friendship and mine began at an earlier date. It accompanied us thro' long and important scenes. The different conclusions we had drawn from our political reading and reflections were not permitted to lessen mutual esteem, each party being conscious they were the result of an honest conviction in the other. Like differences of opinion existing among our fellow citizens attached them to the one or the other of us, and produced a rivalship in their minds which did not exist in ours. We never stood in one another's way: for it either had been withdrawn at any time, his favorers would not have gone over to the other, but would have sought for some one of homogeneous opinions. This consideration was sufficient to keep down all jealousy between us, and to guard our friendship from any disturbance by sentiments of rivalship: and I can say with truth that one act of Mr. Adams's life, and one only, ever gave me a moment's personal displeasure. I did consider his last appointments to office as personally unkind. They were from among my most ardent political enemies, from whom no faithful cooperation could ever be expected, and laid me under the embarrasment of acting thro' men whose views were to defeat mine; or to encounter the odium of putting others in their places. It seemed but common justice to leave a successor free to act by instruments of his own choice. If my respect for him did not permit me to ascribe the whole blame to the influence of others, it left something for friendship to forgive, and after brooding over it for some little time, and not always resisting the expression of it, I forgave it cordially, and returned to the same state of esteem and respect for him which had so long subsisted. Having come into life a little later than Mr. Adams, his career has preceded mine, as mine is followed by some other, and it will probably be closed at the same distance after him which time originally placed between us. I maintain for him, and shall carry into private life an uniform and high measure of respect and good will, and for yourself a sincere attachment. I have thus, my dear Madam, opened myself to you without reserve, which I have long wished an opportunity of doing; and, without knowing how it will be received, I feel relief from being unbosomed. And I have now only to entreat your forgiveness for this transition from a subject of domestic affliction to one which seems of a different aspect. But tho connected with political events, it has been viewed by me most strongly in it's unfortunate bearings on my private friendships. The injury these have sustained has been a heavy price for what has never given me equal pleasure. That you may both be favored with health, tranquility and long life, is the prayer of one who tenders you the assurances of his highest consideration and esteem.

Th: Jefferson

[Cappon, pp. 268-271]

Liberty for God's Chosen People

History remembers our fourth president, James Madison (1751-1836), as the father of the United States Constitution. A Virginia native, he spent his life in service to his fellow citizens, first in state government, where he helped secure passage of Thomas Jefferson's religious freedom bill, and then on the national level as a U.S. congressman, secretary of state under Jefferson and president from 1809-1817.

A popular chief executive, Madison was regarded highly by the people for his contribution to the establishment of religious freedom in America. Even after he left office, Madison received letters thanking him for his efforts, including a letter from an obscure man named Jacob de la Motta, who may have been a Southern rabbi. In his response, Madison offered his thoughts on the subject.

"Among the features peculiar to the Political system of the United States, is the perfect equality of rights which it secures to every religious Sect."

August, 1820

Dear Friend,

I have received your letter of the 7th inst. with the Discourse delivered at the Consecration of the Hebrew Synagogue at Savannah, for which you will please to accept my thanks.

95

The history of the Jews must forever be interesting. The modern part of it is, at the same time so little generally known, that every ray of light on the subject has its value.

Among the features peculiar to the Political system of the United States, is the perfect equality of rights which it secures to every religious Sect. And it is particularly pleasing to observe in the good citizenship of such as have been most distrusted and oppressed elsewhere, a happy illustration of the safety and success of this experiment of a just and benignant policy. Equal laws protecting equal rights, are found as they ought to be presumed, the best guarantee of loyalty and love of country; as well as best calculated to cherish that mutual respect and good will among Citizens of every religious denomination which are necessary to social harmony and most favorable to the advancement of truth. The account you give of the Jews of your Congregation brings them fully within the scope of those observations.

[Cousins, pp. 320-321]

4

A Rising Storm:
Letters of the Pre-Civil War Period

THE EVENTS THAT led to the Civil War could be described as resulting from the "unfinished business" of the American Revolution. The Constitutional declaration that "all men are created equal and endowed by their Creator with certain inalienable rights" was destined to clash with racist practices, of which Americans from every region were guilty. Many of the letters during this era reflect Christian principles in dealing with others, even in the midst of a time of moral confusion.

"My great and beloved Father"

Andrew Jackson (1767-1845) became the seventh President of the United States in 1828. A man with extensive experience in dealing with Native Americans, "Old Hickory" relentlessly removed Indian tribes further to the west of the Mississippi River during his two terms. In 1832 he received a poignant, well-argued letter from Levi Colbert, Principal Chief of Oklahoma's Chickasaw Indians, and an old acquaintance. Colbert explained why the treaty proposed by the U.S. Government was so unjust to his people who lived in the Northern Mississippi and Southern Tennessee regions. In the lengthy missive Colbert frequently appealed to the Christian character of America to strengthen his arguments. His plea went unheeded, however, and the removal of the Chickasaws to modern-day Oklahoma began in earnest five years later.

"I saw the whitemans march was to take my country. I prepared my mind and the mind of my Nation for it."

Chickasaw Nation
Nov. 22d 1832

To the President of the United States
My great and beloved Father

As the head of my Nation, my heart tells me it is right that I place truth before you and if you have looked me in the face and dealt with my heart often

99

and long enough, to credit my words, you shall have truth in its nakedness. I had not lived and cast my senses, as you know, along the whitemans march, with my eyes shut, man proves the hand of God can no more change principles fixed in him, than he can change his skin, so it is, with the Indian, and his native land, when he hears of a departure from it, his heart like the stricken deer, reels and falls, but he may not die. I saw the whitemans march was to take my country. I prepared my mind and the mind of my Nation for it. . . .

My Father—I beg the President and the Senate to consider of the losses, expenses and difficulties, My Nation must meet in removing to the west, this question [k]nows from its nature can't be counters, but to a whole Nation is appalling. The Chickasaw feel a native born attachment for their Country and it seems to me true, that nature presents nothing in the west, which can make the Chickasaws more happy there—than here, their Native and beloved land. It is true that my Nation become willing to see their Country, to put down that bitter question of State sovereignty, to keep peace in the white family, to preserve the Union of the United States whose friendship and protection we want, and our selves, to get away from the troubles which our white brothers fixed upon us. It is the result of our weakness and we surrender our Country to cure the evils we never created. The whole question considered, to us it seems right that the United States pay the Chickasaws one hundred thousand dollars as asked for in their treaty. We hope that our father the President and Senate will think with us and afford their powerful aid, this will help soften the Chickasaw hearts. Convince them of the liberality and Justice of the United States, and promote the brother hood of the white and red men in the west.

My great and beloved father, the whole Chickasaw Nation, by my heart and my mouth, in this last attempted bargain, for their last foot of land within the United States, beg leave to speak as they feel. My whole Nation is deeply dissatisfied with Genl. Coffees treaty, for remedy, we do not Cast ourselves into the arms your Enemys, but like true and faithful children, we come first to you and bring our complaints to our fathers wisdom and justice, we ask of him to except of our treaty of this date, with which my whole Nation will be satisfied and strong friends as they always have been.

My father, at the treaty at Pontetoc, we were shorn of our friends, of our lands and of the government we always lov'd, our country, lov'd for ages, by one treaty of the other, is gone. Soon to blaze with the white mans fires and my Nation again must kindle a feeble light in the wilds where the ax nor the hoe has never been heard, but my father will do us justice now and let us part in peace, so that I may have truth in my mouth and may say to my people in the west, altho it was necessary for the happiness of the United States to have our old Country, yet General Jackson and the Senate, has been honest, Just and liberal. . . .

The inside dress which the Almighty Cherishes, and gives to true greatness, all its action and all its immortality, these in the American character tells to the world that—that liberty, which God gave and

Washington left, has no security any further than this uprightness and just benevolence acts on and governs community.

> Truly your old and constant friend
> Levi Colbert, Principal chief of the Chickasaws
>
> [Armstrong, Kerry]

Birthday Admonitions to a Future Leader

The most famous of all the New England Alcotts is, of course, Louisa May, the author of the beloved classic Little Women. *However, in his day her father, Bronson (1799-1888), was renowned for his work as an unconventional educator and writer. He established a school that dared admit a black girl, which led to its failure, and in the mid-1840s set up a utopian community outside Boston which was dedicated to vegetarianism. It lasted less than a year. Settling down in Concord, Massachusetts with his family, Bronson Alcott earned an appointment as superintendent of schools in 1857. During that time he created educational innovations including the parent-teacher association.*

Alcott was an educator extraordinaire who did not confine his instruction to the schools he supervised or their students; he also seized opportunities to instruct his own offspring in the ways he deemed best, especially on birthdays. On Louisa May's seventh, she received this letter from him. It was unlike any store-bought card of our times, encouraging the child to "whoop it up" on her day of days. Rather, it was an admonition to grow more mature to accompany the increase of her years, specifically to learn to listen to and heed her God-given conscience.

"You feel your conscience, and have no real pleasure unless you obey it. You cannot love yourself, or any one else, when you do not mind its Commandments."

(Boston, November 29, 1839)

For Louisa 1839.
My Daughter,

You are Seven years old to day, and your Father is forty. You have learned a great many things, since you have lived in a Body, about things going on around you, and within you. You know how to think, how to resolve, how to love and how to obey. You feel your CONSCIENCE, and have no real pleasure unless you obey it. You cannot love yourself, or any one else, when you do not mind its Commandments. It asks you always to BE GOOD, and bears, O how gently! how patiently! with all endeavors to hate, and treat it cruelly. How kindly it bears with you all the while! How sweetly it whispers Happiness in your HEART when you Obey its soft words. How it smiles upon you, and makes you Glad when you Resolve to Obey it! How terrible its Punishments! It is GOD trying in your SOUL to keep you always Good.

You begin, my dear daughter, another year this morning. Your Father, your Mother, and Sisters, with your little friends, show their love on this your Birth-Day, by giving you this BOX: Open it, and take what is in it; and the best wishes of

> Your Father.
> Beach Street,
> Friday Morning, Nov. 29,
> 183[9]

[Herrnstadt, p. 43]

The Tender Side of a Stone Wall

Thomas J. "Stonewall" Jackson (1824-1863) is remembered primarily as a man of war. An 1846 graduate of West Point, he became professor of natural and experimental philosophy (a subject roughly equivalent to physics) and instructor of artillery at Virginia's Military Institute. When war broke out between the states, Jackson became a brigadier general in the Confederate Army. Jackson earned his famous nickname while his soldiers held off a strong Union assault and he stood "like a stone wall" at the battle of First Bull Run in 1861.

The lanky commander was, however, a deeply committed Christian whose tenderness toward his wife was surpassed only by his great love for Christ. He wrote this letter to his beloved Anna before their marriage in 1857.

"As my mind dwells on you, I love to give it a devotional turn, by thinking of you as a gift from our Heavenly Father."

Dear Anna,

In my daily walks I think much of you. I love to stroll abroad after the labors of the day are over, and indulge feelings of gratitude to God for all the sources of natural beauty with which he has adorned the earth. . . . As my mind dwells on you, I love to give it a devotional turn, by thinking of you as a gift from our Heavenly Father. . . .

I wish I could be with you tomorrow at your communion . . . my prayer will be for your growth in every Christian grace. . . It is to me a great satisfaction that our Heavenly Father has so manifestly ordered our union. . . When in prayer for you last Sabbath, the tears came to my eyes and I realized an unusual degree of emotional tenderness. I have not yet fully analyzed my feelings to my satisfaction, so as to arrive at the cause of such emotions; but I am disposed to think that it consisted in the idea of the intimate relation existing between you, as the object of my tender affection, and God, to whom I looked up as my Heavenly Father. I felt that as if it were a communion day for myself. . . .

[Davis, pp. 123-124]

A Zealous Abolitionist's Last Letter

Today's press would undoubtedly label John Brown (1800-1859) an extremist. He was, in fact, so zealously devoted to abolitionism that he advocated violence against slavery's supporters, a conviction that took hold during his Ohio youth. As a young man, Brown devoted his life to a crusade against slavery. Toward the end of it, he organized a plan to invade the South in order to provoke a massive slave rebellion.

In 1859 Brown led a raid on Harper's Ferry, West Virginia. Although he and his twenty-one men seized the federal arsenal, there was no slave insurrection, and the small band of zealots found themselves trapped inside. A contingent of U.S. Marines, led by Col. Robert E. Lee, captured Brown and the surviving members of his band. The abolitionist was sentenced to hang.

On November 30, 1859, the night before he was executed, Brown wrote to his family from the Charleston prison in Jefferson County, Virginia. He said that he had acted according to his convictions.

"My dear younger children will you listen to the last poor admonition of one who can only love you? Oh be determined at once to give your whole hearts to God; & let nothing shake; or alter; that resolution."

My Dearly Beloved Wife, Sons: & Daughters, Everyone

As I now begin what is probably the last letter I shall ever write to any of you; I conclude to write you all at the same time. . . . I am waiting the hour of my public murder with great composure of mind, & cheerfulness: feeling the strongest assurance that in no other possible way could I be used to so much advance the cause of God; & of humanity: & that nothing that either I or all my family have sacrificed or suffered: will be lost.

The reflection that a wise & merciful, as well as just & holy God: rules not only the affairs of this world; but of all worlds; is a rock to set our feet upon; under all circumstances: even those more severely trying ones: into which our own follies; & wrongs have placed us. I have now no doubt but that our seeming disaster: will ultimately result in the most glorious success. So my dear shattered & broken family be of good cheer; & believe & trust in God; "with all your heart & with all your soul;" for "he doeth ALL things well." Do not feel ashamed on my account; nor for one moment despair of the cause; or grow weary of well doing. I bless God; I never felt stronger confidence in the certain and near approach of a bright Morning; & a glorious day; than I have felt; & do now feel; since my confinement here.

I am endeavoring to "return" like a "poor Prodigal" as I am, to my Father: against whom I have always sinned: in the hope; that he may kindly, & forgivingly "meet me: though a very great way off."

A Rising Storm

Oh my dear Wife & Children would "to God" you could know how I have been "travelling in birth for you" all: that no one of you "may fail of the grace of God, through Jesus Christ:" that no one of you may be blind to the truth: & glorious "light of his word," in which Life; & Immortality; are brought to light.

I beseech you every one to make the bible your dayly & Nightly study; with a childlike honest, candid, teachable spirit: out of love and respect for your husband; & Father: & I beseech the God of my Fathers; to open all your eyes to a discovery of the truth. You cannot imagine how much you may soon need the consolations of the Christian religion. . . .

Oh do not trust your eternal all upon the boisterous Ocean, without even a Helm; or Compass to aid you in steering. I do not ask any of you; to throw away your reason: I only ask you, to make a candid & sober use of your reason: My dear younger children will you listen to the last poor admonition of one who can only love you? Oh be determined at once to give your whole hearts to God; & let nothing shake; or alter; that resolution. You need have no fear of regreting it. . . .

Be faithful unto death. From the exercise of habitual love to man: it cannot be very hard: to learn to love his maker. I must yet insert a reason for my firm belief in the Divine inspiration of the Bible: notwithstanding I am (perhaps naturally) skeptical: (certainly not, credulous.) I wish you all to consider it most thoroughly; when you read the blessed book; & see whether you can not discover such evidence yourselves. it is the purity of heart, feeling or motive: as well as word, & action which is everywhere insisted

109

on; that distinguish it from all other teachings; that commends it to my conscience; whether my heart be "willing, & obedient" or not. The inducement that it hold out; are another reason of my conviction of its truth: & genuineness: that I cannot here omit; in this my last argument for the Bible.

Eternal life; is what my soul is "panting after" this moment. I mention this; as reason for endeavoring to leave a valuable copy of the Bible to be carefully preserved in remembrance of me: to so many of my posterity; instead of some other things of equal cost. . . .

Be determined to know by experience as soon as may be: whether bible instruction is of Divine origin or not; which says; "Owe no man anything but to love one another." John Rogers wrote to his children, "Abhor the arrant whore of Rome." John Brown writes to his children to abhor with undiing hatred, also: that "sum of all vilainies;" Slavery.

Remember that "he that is slow to anger is better than the mighty: and he that ruleth his spirit; than he that taketh a city." Remember also: that "they that be wise shall shine; and they that turn many to righteousness: as the stars forever; & ever." And now dearly beloved Farewell, To God & the word of his grace I comme(n)d you all.

> Your Affectionate Husband
> & Father
> John Brown
> [Schuster, pp. 335-338]

5

Brother Against Brother:
Letters of the Civil War Period

THE CIVIL WAR, complex in its origins, was fought over more issues than slavery, although that certainly was the most visible and emotional one. That is at least one reason why, despite the fact that evangelicals were in the forefront of the abolitionist movement, Christian believers were on both sides of the conflict. Dividing friends, families and churches, the war tore the fabric of society and visited unbelievable carnage on a nation yet to celebrate its centennial. The letters that follow reflect the divided loyalties of the time and, for some, the knowledge of a Rock of safety in the storm.

Friendship Across Battle Lines

A West Point graduate, Jefferson Davis (1808-1889) was a soldier in the Mexican War before becoming a Congressman from Mississippi. He also served as the U.S. Secretary of War under President Franklin Pierce and as a United States Senator. There came a time, however, when he broke away from the Union because of his convictions about states' rights and slavery.

Just before assuming the Presidency of the Confederate States of America, Davis wrote a poignant letter to his close companion, Franklin Pierce, informing him that their friendship was about to enter a most difficult period.

"Civil war has only horror for me, but whatever circumstances demand shall be met as a duty and I trust be so discharged that you will not be ashamed of our former connection or cease to be my friend."

Washington D.C.
Jany. 20. 1861

My dear friend,

I have often and sadly turned my thoughts to you during the troublous times through which we have been passing and now I come to the hard task of announcing to you that the hour is at hand which closes my connection with the United States, for the independence and Union of which my Father bled and in the service of which I have sought to emulate the example he set for my guidance. Mississippi not as a matter of choice but of necessity has resolved to enter on the trial of secession. Those who have driven her to this alternative threaten to deprive her of the right to require that her government shall rest on the consent of the governed, to substitute foreign force for domestic support, to reduce a state to the condition from which the colony rose. In the attempt to avoid the issue which had been joined by the country, the present Administration has complicated and precipitated the question. Even now if the duty "to preserve the public property" was rationally regarded the probable collision at Charleston would be avoided. Security far better than any which the federal troops can give might be obtained in consideration of the little garrison of Fort Sumpter. If the disavowal of any purpose to coerce So. Ca. be sincere the possession of a work to command the harbor is worse than useless.

When Lincoln comes in he will have but to continue in the path of his predecessor to inaugurate a civil war and, leave a *soi disant* democratic administration responsible for the fact. Genl. [Caleb] Cushing was here last week and when we parted it seemed like taking a last leave of a Brother.

I leave immediately for Missi. and know not what may devolve upon me after my return. Civil war has only horror for me, but whatever circumstances demand shall be met as a duty and I trust be so discharged that you will not be ashamed of our former connection or cease to be my friend.

I had hoped this summer to have had an opportunity to see you and Mrs. Pierce and to have shown to you our children. Mrs. Davis was sorely disappointed when we turned Southward without seeing you, I believe she wrote to Mrs. Pierce in explanation of the circumstances which prevented us from executing our cherished plan of a visit to you when we should leave West Point.

Mrs. Davis joins me in kindest remembrance to Mrs. Pierce and the expression of the hope that we may yet have you both at our country home. Do me the favor to write to me often, address Hurricane P.O. Warren County, Missi.

May God bless you is ever the prayer of your friend.

Jefferson Davis

[J. Davis, pp. 17-18]

"My love for you is deathless . . ."

In 1990 historian Ken Burns presented a ground-breaking television documentary about the Civil War. At the end of the first episode, actor Paul Roebling read a moving letter from Union Major Sullivan Ballou to his wife just seven days before he died at the first battle of Bull Run. He writes in the letter of his great love for the nation, a dedication so profound that it could take him away from his darling Sarah without regret.

"If I do not [survive] my dear Sarah, never forget how much I love you, and when my last breath escapes me on the battlefield, it will whisper your name. . . . Sarah do not mourn me dead; think I am gone and wait for thee, for we shall meet again."

July 14, 1861
Camp Clark, Washington

My very dear Sarah:

The indications are very strong that we shall move in a few days—perhaps tomorrow. Lest I should not be able to write again, I feel impelled to write a few lines that may fall under your eye when I shall be no more . . .

I have no misgivings about, or lack of confidence in the cause in which I am engaged, and my courage does not halt or falter. I know how strongly American

Civilization now leans on the triumph of the Government, and how great a debt we owe to those who went before us through the blood and sufferings of the Revolution. And I am willing—perfectly willing—to lay down all my joys in this life, to help maintain this Government, and to pay that debt . . . .

Sarah my love for you is deathless, it seems to bind me with mighty cables that nothing but Omnipotence could break; and yet my love of Country comes over me like a strong wind and bears me unresistibly on with all these chains to the battle field.

The memories of the blissful moments I have spent with you come creeping over me, and I feel most gratified to God and to you that I have enjoyed them so long. And hard it is for me to give them up and burn to ashes the hopes of future years, when, God willing, we might still have lived and loved together, and seen our sons grown up to honorable manhood, around us. I have, I know, but few small claims upon Divine Providence, but something whispers to me—perhaps it is the wafted prayer of my little Edgar, that I shall return to my loved ones unharmed. If I do not my dear Sarah, never forget how much I love you, and when my last breath escapes me on the battle field, it will whisper your name. forgive my many faults, and the pains I have caused you. How thoughtless and foolish I have often times been! How gladly would I wash out with my tears every little spot upon your happiness . . . Sarah do not mourn me dead; think I am gone and wait for thee, for we shall meet again.

["The Civil War." Copyright 1990, PBS]

A Confederate Soldier's Faith

Ted Barclay (1844-1915) was born in Lexington, Virginia, home of Virginia Military Institute, and served for four years in the Liberty Hall Volunteers of the fabled Stonewall Brigade. He proudly counted among his ancestors two who served in the American Revolution. As a soldier himself, he found himself in the thick of important Civil War battles: First Manassas (Bull Run), Chancellorsville, Gettysburg. After Barclay received a promotion for gallantry at the battle of Mine Run, the Union Army took him captive at Spotsylvania Court House where he spent the rest of the war. He was released in July 1865 and went home to Lexington where he took his place as a community leader.

Young Barclay was a Christian gentleman whose ardent wish was to go home alive, unless God willed otherwise. He did get his wish, but only after enduring fifteen months in the badly crowded federal prison on a marshy Delaware River island. Barclay spent the rest of his life as a farmer, newspaper editor, political activist, district supervisor and businessman. He also served as deacon and ruling elder for forty-six years in his Presbyterian church and was on the board of trustees of Washington and Lee University.

As a youth in the army, Barclay made a profession of faith "in the field" (p. 8). In a February 10, 1864 letter to his parents, the depth of his faith in God in the midst of harsh uncertainty and temptation, a faith that would guide him throughout his illustrious life, shone through brightly.

"I do from my heart believe that I have been brought to a saving knowledge of Jesus Christ and though I am exposed to great temptations still His grace is sufficient for me."

Dear Homefolks,

You no doubt have imagined that I have forgotten you, and that the Yanks have gotten me, but neither is the case. I have just returned from an eight day picket on the Rapid Ann where it was impossible to write, and though I feel somewhat tired will endeavor to write tonight for the mail tomorrow.

I have received two letters since my arrival in camp. . . . The (second) letter was from Mother, which I have just finished reading. I am very thankful to you for your excellent advice. Do you think that I could for one moment think of returning to the beggarly elements of this world after enjoying the sweets of this Christian life?

I do from my heart believe that I have been brought to a saving knowledge of Jesus Christ and though I am exposed to great temptations still His grace is sufficient for me and I never cease to pray that He will keep me in the straight and narrow path that leadest to heaven, and I trust and believe that you never lift up your heart to the mercy seat of God without remembering your absent son. And has He not promised to hear our prayers?

Oh, do not for one moment believe that I could be induced to forsake the cause of Christ; it is the only thing that sheds any light on this dark cloud of war, the only thing that smooths my rugged pathway. I will ever endeavor to fix my eyes upon the cross of Christ as a mariner to his needle, until I shall safely arrive at last in heaven. The life of a Christian must be dear to anyone, but how doubly dear it is to a soldier. How sweet it is to feel that I am a Christian when all is dark and gloomy around me. The light that emanates from the Cross of Christ drives away this gloom and makes my heart so light and happy. What perfect happiness we sometimes feel, but the devil tempts us and we do not always feel so.

Oh, that we were all Christians. Then this cloud of war would pass away, and the bright rainbow of peace would soon shoot across our political sky; but our people seem to have all gone astray and riches seem to be their only thought, so they are not exposed to the fury of war, they care very little for the poor soldiers. But thank God there are some who think of us, some whose thoughts are turned to the absent ones far, far away from home, and how dear is the thought that they think of us. Even now your thoughts may be of me and your prayers ascending to heaven in my behalf. I thank God for these kind and loving friends and, though separated from them, our imaginations can call us their loved forms and faces.

I have just had another manifestation of His mercy towards me in being safely spared through the battle of another day. Though it was not a severe fight, it requires only one ball to end our lives and many a one passed harmlessly by.

That is the time it is to feel how sweet it is to be a Christian. When the balls are flying thick around you and dealing death all around, to commit yourself into His care, that He has power to hurl by harmless the missiles of death. As an old Christian warrior once said, "every bullet has its billet," I think is eminently true.

But as I am sleepy and tired, I will close. You have no doubt seen a better description of the late fight than I can give. I may give you my official report in the next. Excuse this scratch. I believe I am getting more careless about my writing every day, but I console myself by saying that all great men wrote badly.

> Give my love to all friends,
> Yours affectionately,
> A.T.B.

[Turner, pp. 123-126]

"i am free"

As the War Between the States pierced the nation's spirit with its venom, some Southern slaves escaped to the North where they joined special Union regiments. Born in slavery in Maryland, a black man named John Boston made it safely across the Mason-Dixon line and became the servant of a Union officer. This letter to his wife tells of his hard-fought and deeply cherished freedom, as well as his sadness that they were apart. From the labored way in which he wrote, one can discern that his education was rudimentary at best.

"I had a little truble in giting away But as the Lord led the Children of Isrel to the land of Canon So he lef me to a land Whare fredom Will rain in spite Of earth and hell . . . i am free from al the Slavers Lash."

Upton Hill (Virginia)
January the 12, 1862

My Dear Wife

it is with grate joy I take this time to let you know Whare I am i am now in Safety in the 14th Regiment of Brooklyn this Day i can Address you thank God as a free man I had a little truble in giting away But as the Lord led the Children of Isrel to the land of Canon So he lef me to a land Whare fredom Will rain in spite Of earth and hell Dear you must make your Self content i am free from al the Slavers Lash and as you have chose the Wise plan Of Serving the Lord i hope you Will pray much and i Will try by the help of god To Serv him With all my hart I am With a very nice man and have All that hart Can Wish But My Dear I Cant express my grate desire that i Have to See you i trust the time Will Come When We Shal meet again And if We don't met on earth We Will Meet in heven Whare Jesas ranes Dear Elizabeth tell Mrs Own(ess) That i trust that She Will Continue Her kindness to you and that god Will Bless her on earth and Save her In grate eternity My Acomplements To Mrs Owens and her Children may They Prosper through life I never Shall forgit her kindness to me Dear Wife i must Close rest yourself Contented i am free i Want you to rite To me Soon as you Can Without Delay Direct your letter to the 14th Regiment New york State malitia Uptons Hill Virginear In Care of Mr Cranford Comary Write my Dear Soon As you C[an] Your Affectionate Husban Kiss Daniel For me

> John Boston
> Give my love to Father and
> Mother
> [Berlin, p. 189]

Letters of Abraham Lincoln

Although he is considered one of the greatest Americans ever to have lived, Abraham Lincoln (1809-1865) knew what it was like to fail. The Kentucky-born statesman became an Illinois state legislator in 1835, a post at which he did not distinguish himself. A successful lawyer following that bland experience, he became a United States Congressman in 1847. As with his previous political experience, that only lasted for two years. In 1858 Lincoln lost a bid for the Senate to Stephen A. Douglas, a pro-slavery Democrat.

He never gave up, though. While he may have lost the opportunity to become a U.S. Senator, the lanky lawyer had gained a national reputation from the lively debates between him and Douglas. In 1860 he won the presidency. That prompted the secession of the Southern states from the Union that he fought mightily to restore over the next four years, an effort that eventually cost him his life.

Encouraging a War-Weary General

An able commander-in-chief, Lincoln took a direct interest in conducting the war effort. He hired and fired generals and visited Northern troops on the front lines. One Army commander who arrested the President's attention was a man somewhat like himself, Ulysses S. Grant, who had shown flashes of greatness in his younger years, combined with rather dismal periods. In the opening year of the Civil War, Grant took a commission as a colonel, but he so distinguished himself in battle that, recognizing his military genius, Lincoln promoted him to general.

In April, 1864, a year after he started commanding the entire Union effort, Grant received a letter from Pres-

ident Lincoln expressing his utmost trust in Grant's ability to continue leading the Union troops, in spite of an enemy that just wouldn't quit.

"The particulars of your plans I neither know or seek to know. You are vigilant and self-reliant; and, pleased with this, I wish not to obtrude any constraints or restraints upon you."

Executive Mansion
Washington, April 30. 1864.

Lieutenant General Grant.

Not expecting to see you again before the Spring campaign opens, I wish to express, in this way, my entire satisfaction with what you have done up to this time, so far as I understand it. The particulars of your plans I neither know or seek to know. You are vigilant and self-reliant; and, pleased with this, I wish not to obtrude any constraints or restraints upon you. While I am very anxious that any great disaster, or capture of our men in great numbers, shall be avoided, I know these points are less likely to escape your attention than they would be mine. If there is anything wanting which is within my power to give, do not fail to let me know it.

And now with a brave army, and a just cause, may God sustain you.

Yours very truly
A. Lincoln

[Basler, pp. 750-751]

The Little Peoples' Petition

In April 1864 a petition and about two dollars reached President Abraham Lincoln's desk at the White House. One hundred ninety-five children had signed the entreaty, asking the Chief Executive to free the slave children in the South. (The Emancipation Proclamation had gone into effect on January 1, 1863, but its practical effects south of the Mason-Dixon line were nil. The Thirteenth Amendment that legally ended slavery was passed in 1865.)

Referred to by Lincoln as the "Little People's Petition," the document went over the endorsement of Mrs. Horace Mann, widow of the famous educator. As President, Lincoln faced continual pressure between those in the North who thought he had gone too far to end slavery and those who asserted that he hadn't gone nearly far enough.

In response he penned a thank you letter and sent it straightaway to Mrs. Mann through Senator Charles Sumner. This came to the woman as a surprise because the use of her name on the petition was, she said "wholly without my knowledge." She quickly added, "I cannot regret it, since it has given me this precious note from your hand" (Holzer, p. 102).

Executive Mansion,
Washington, April 5, 1864.

Mrs. Horace Mann,
Madam,

The petition of persons under eighteen, praying that I would free all slave children, and the heading of which petition it appears you wrote, was handed me a few days since by Senator Sumner. Please tell these little people I am very glad their young hearts are so full of just and generous sympathy, and that, while I have not the power to grant all they ask, I trust they will remember that God has, and that, it seems, He wills to do it. Yours truly

A. Lincoln

[Holzer, p. 102]

A Farewell to His Readers

The Liberator, *begun in 1831 by William Lloyd Garrison (1805-1879), became the nation's most influential abolitionist newspaper. It was Garrison's second attempt at publishing an antislavery journal; his first came in 1829 when he and partner Benjamin Lundy produced the monthly* Genius of Universal Emancipation. *Because it was Baltimore-based, however, and that city operated as a center of the slave trade, Garrison moved to a more sympathetic town, Boston. There he and Isaac Knapp launched* The Liberator.

Garrison believed that freeing the slaves would be putting Christian principles to work; indeed, his convictions were an outworking of his faith. Over the years Garrison received death threats and cruel letters because of his efforts to abolish slavery, and the state of Georgia once offered a $5,000 reward for his arrest and conviction. He persisted, however, in spite of great opposition, until the Union victory in the War Between the States ensured the emancipation of the slaves. His mission accomplished, Garrison wrote this letter to his readers in the last issue of The Liberator *on December 29, 1865.*

"Better to be always in a minority of one with God—branded as madman, incendiary, fanatic, heretic, infidel . . . in defence of the right, than like Herod, having the shouts of a multitude, crying, 'It is the voice of a god, and not of a man!' "

THE LAST NUMBER OF *THE LIBERATOR*

> The last! the last! the last!
> O, by that little word
> How many thoughts are
>   stirred—
> That sister of THE PAST!

The present number of the *Liberator* is the completion of its thirty-fifth volume, and the termination of its existence. . . .

I began the publication of the *Liberator* without a subscriber, and I end it—it gives me unalloyed satisfaction to say—without a farthing as the pecuniary result of the patronage extended to it during the thirty-five years of unremitted labors.

From the immense change wrought in the national feeling and sentiment on the subject of slavery, the *Liberator* derived no advantage at any time in regard to its circulation. The original "disturber of the peace," nothing was left undone at the beginning, and up to the hour of the late rebellion, by Southern slaveholding villainy on the one hand, and Northern pro-slavery malice on the other, to represent it as too vile a sheet to be countenanced by any claiming to be Christian or patriotic; and it always required rare moral courage or singular personal independence to be among its patrons. Never had a journal to look such opposition in the face—never was one so constantly belied and caricatured. If it had advocated all the crimes forbidden by the moral law of God and the statutes of the State, instead of vindicating the sacred claims of oppressed and bleeding humanity, it could not have been more vehemently denounced or more indignantly repudiated. To this day— such is the force of prejudice—there are multitudes who cannot be induced to read a single number of it, even on the score of curiosity, though their views on the slavery question are now precisely those which it has uniformly advocated. Yet no journal has been conducted with such fairness and impartiality; none has so scrupulously and uniformly presented all sides of every question discussed in its pages; none has so readily and exhaustively published, without note or comment, what its enemies have said to its disparagement, and the vilification of its editor; none has vindicated primitive Christianity, in its spirit and purpose—"the higher law," in its supremacy over nations and governments as well as individual conscience—the Golden Rule, in its binding obligation upon all classes—the Declaration of Independence, with its self-evident truths— the rights of human nature, without distinction of race, complexion or sex—more earnestly or more uncompromisingly; none has exerted a higher moral or more broadly reformatory influence upon those who have given it a careful perusal; and none has gone beyond it in asserting the Fatherhood of God and the brotherhood of man. All this may be claimed for it without egotism or presumption. It has ever been "a terror to evil-doers, and a praise to them that do well."

It has excited the fierce hostility of all that is vile and demoniacal in the land, and won the affection and regard of the purest and noblest of the age. To me it has been unspeakably cheering, and the richest compensation for whatever or peril, suffering and defamation I have been called to encounter, that one uniform testimony has been borne, by those who have had its weekly perusal, as to the elevating and quickening influence of the *Liberator* upon their character and lives; and the deep grief they are expressing in view of its discontinuance is overwhelmingly affecting to my feelings. None of these date their subscription from the commencement of the paper, and they have allowed nothing in its columns to pass without a rigid scrutiny. They speak, therefore, experimentally, and "testify of that which they have seen and do know." Let them be assured that my regret in the separation which is to take place between us, in consequence of the discontinuance of the *Liberator*, is at least as poignant as their own; and let them feel, as I do, comforted by the thought that it relates only to the weekly method of communicating with each other, and not to the principles we have espoused in the past, or the hopes and aims we cherish as to the future.

Although the *Liberator* was designed to be, and has ever been, mainly devoted to the abolition of slavery, yet it has been instrumental in aiding the cause of reform in many of its most important aspects. . . .

I see a mighty work of enlightenment and regeneration yet to be accomplished at the South, and many cruel wrongs done to the freedmen which are yet to be redressed; and I neither counsel others to turn away from the field of conflict, under the delusions that no more remains to be done, nor contemplate such a course in my own case.

The object for which the *Liberator* was commenced—the extermination of chattel slavery—having been gloriously consummated, it seems to me specially appropriate to let its existence cover the historic period of the great struggle; leaving what remains to be done to complete the work of emancipation to other instrumentalities (of which I hope to avail myself) under new auspices, with more abundant means, and with millions instead of hundreds for allies.

Most happy am I to be no longer in conflict with the mass of my fellow-countrymen on the subject of slavery. For no man of any refinement or sensibility can be indifferent to the approbation of his fellow-men, if it be rightly earned. But to obtain it by going with the multitude to do evil—by pandering to despotic power or a corrupt public sentiment—is self-degradation and personal dishonor:

> For more true joy Marcellus exiled feels,
> Than Caesar with a senate at his heels.

Better to be always in a minority of one with God—branded as madman, incendiary, fanatic, heretic, infidel—frowned upon by "the powers that be," and mobbed by the populace—or consigned ignominiously to the gallows, like him whose "soul is marching on," though his "body lies mouldering in the grave," or burnt to ashes at the stake like Wickliffe, or nailed to the cross like him who "gave himself for the world"—in defence of the RIGHT, than like Herod, having the shouts of a multitude, crying, "It is the voice of a god, and not of a man!"

Farewell, tried and faithful patrons! Farewell, generous benefactors, without whose voluntary but essential pecuniary contributions the *Liberator* must have long since been discontinued! Farewell, noble men and women who have wrought so long and so successfully, under God, to break every yoke! Hail, ye ransomed millions! Hail, year of jubilee! With a grateful heart and a fresh baptism of the soul, my last invocation shall be:

> Spirit of Freedom! on—
>   Oh! pause not in thy flight
> Till every clime is won
>   To worship in thy light. . . .

Wm. Lloyd Garrison
Boston, December 29, 1865.
[Ruchames, pp. 245-250]

6

Healing Our Wounds:
Letters of the Post-Civil War Period

"I SEE A MIGHTY work of enlightenment and regeneration yet to be accomplished at the South, and many cruel wrongs done to the freedmen which are yet to be redressed," William Lloyd Garrison prophesied at the end of the Civil War. It was a time for reconsidering attitudes and assumptions, and reforming the patterns of society—in the North as well as in the South. It should not be surprising, then, that it also became a time of revival, beginning with the soldiers during the war and continuing through the heyday of the D.L. Moody campaigns. The following letters tell some of the personal stories behind this time of healing.

Revival in an Army Camp

In the aftermath of the Civil War, Dr. J. William Jones wrote a book entitled Christ in the Camp. *Several clergymen wrote him about the Holy Spirit's work among the troops, letters that Jones included in the appendix of his book. The chaplain of the Thirty-eighth Virginia Infantry, the Reverend R.W. Cridlin, sent this one explaining how God moved in the lives of his men.*

"In this meeting God was with us and His people were revived and more than a hundred converted."

Chesterfield,
March 22, 1867.

Dear Brother Jones:

Before going into details, allow me to state that I was appointed chaplain of the Thirty-eighth Virginia Infantry June 9, 1863, and remained with it to the surrender.

(1.) I am unable to state how many sermons I preached or prayer-meetings held, Bible classes conducted, tracts distributed. I have no record and I can not trust my memory. We had a flourishing Brigade Young Men's Christian Association, and when in camp had our Sabbath-schools and Bible-classes. I know I distributed thousands of tracts, and I have reason to believe much good was done. Just here allow me to relate a little incident illustrating the good effects of tracts. While carrying around these little messengers of love, I entered a tent and found two young men engaged in a game of cards. At first they seemed ashamed, then they braced up their failing courage (if courage it was) and continued the game. I kindly asked "if I could take a hand." Waiting for my turn, I first threw down "Evils of Gaming," then "Mother's Parting Words to her soldier Boy." I found that the game was mine. At the sight of the word "mother," the tears rolled down their cheeks as they both exclaimed: "Parson, I will never play cards again!"

(2.) My first protracted effort was made soon after the battle of Gettysburg, near Orange Court House. In this meeting God was with us and His people were revived and more than a hundred converted. Brother A. Broaddus baptized twenty for me while there. My next meeting (of much interest) was in the fall of 1864, in which about sixty were turned from "darkness to light." I don't remember any remarkable conversions, or that any means were employed beyond the ordinary means of grace.

(3.) Most of those who professed were steadfast in their love and devotion to Christ and His cause. Many of them died in the "triumphs of faith."

(4.) Our first colonel, Colonel Edmunds, was, I think, a member of the Episcopal Church. His influence was very beneficial to his command. I know nothing of his last moments, as he was killed on the field of Gettysburg. Our next colonel was the young yet brave and accomplished gentleman and officer, James Cabell, of Danville. Colonel Cabell was not a member of any Church, but told me a few days before his death "that he felt prepared." He was killed near Drewry's Bluff, May 10, 1864, leaving a young bride and many dear ones to mourn their loss. Colonel George Griggs, of Pittsylvania, was our next colonel. He was a member of the Baptist Church. He was ever ready to aid me in my meetings, and was not ashamed to exhort his men publicly to enlist under the banner of Christ. His life was spared to labor for Christ. Among my most valuable assistants was Captain J.T. Averett. Captain John A. Herndon, Captain Jennings, Captain Grubbs, Lieutenant Gardner and others were true soldiers of Jesus.

General Steuart and his assistant adjutant-general, Captain Darden, were members of the Episcopal Church. Colonel Phillips, of the Ninth, was a man of more than ordinary talent, and he did all he could for Christ.

(5.)It was fully and satisfactorily proved in our regiment that true "soldiers of the Cross" made the best soldiers for their country.

(6.)I don't remember but some four or five who told me that they would devote the rest of their time to the ministry. Captain J.A. Herndon, of Pittsylvania, of the Methodist Episcopal Church expected to do so. Brother W.A. Morefield, of Halifax; Brother Hodges, Methodist Episcopal; Brother C. Penick, Episcopal Church; Brother C.F. James (Captain Company F, Eighth Virginia), of Loudon, whom I baptized, is now at Richmond College preparing himself for the ministry. No doubt many others will decide to "go and do likewise." God grant it.

(7.) I baptized about forty. I was not ordained till December, 1863. I think I can safely put the whole number of conversions in the brigade at 500, as other chaplains had gracious revivals, and have reason to infer they had many conversions.

My dear brother, you have my best wishes and prayers in your arduous work. We need such a book. I think it will do much good. If I can serve you in any way, I am at your service. May the Lord bless us at an early date with such refreshing showers of grace as we enjoyed in Orange in 1863.

Yours in Christian love,
R.W. Cridlin

[Farley, pp. 13-14]

"Dear Friend Phillips"

Massachusetts-born Lydia Maria Child (1802-1880) spent her life teaching, writing and pursuing social reform. In addition to several popular books, she published the nation's first monthly children's magazine, Juvenile Miscellany. *She became an ardent abolitionist after her future husband, David, introduced her to William Lloyd Garrison in 1828, the same year of her marriage. Boston society shunned Mrs. Child after she published "An Appeal in Favor of That Class of Americans Called Africans," a document in which she promoted the education of blacks. Sales of her books also fell off when she wrote an antislavery pamphlet in 1833, but for the rest of her life she never backed away from supporting causes in which she strongly believed.*

Like many abolitionists, Mrs. Child lived to see the slaves emancipated. She realized, however, that although blacks were legally free, their struggle to attain true equality continued.

In this 1868 letter to a certain Mr. Phillips of the American Antislavery Society, Lydia and her husband assessed the post-Civil War condition of African-Americans.

"To us the present crisis of the country seems more dangerous than [before the Civil War]. . . . The insidiousness of oppressors is always more to be dreaded than their open violence. There can be no reasonable doubt that a murderous feeling toward the colored people prevails. . . ."

Wayland, Jan. 1st, 1868.

Dear Friend Phillips:—We enclose $50 as our subscription to the Anti-slavery Society. If our means equalled our wishes, we would send a sum as large as the legacy Francis Jackson intended for that purpose, and of which the society was deprived, as we think, by an unjust legal decision. If our sensible and judicious friend could speak to us from the other side of Jordan, we doubt not he would say that the vigilance of the Anti-slavery Society was never more needed than at the present crisis, and that consequently, he was never more disposed to aid it liberally.

Of course the rancorous pride and prejudice of this country cannot be cured by any short process, not even by lessons so sternly impressive as those of our recent bloody conflict. There is cause for great thankfulness that "war Abolitionists" were driven to perform so important a part in the great program of Providence; but their recognition of human brotherhood is rarely of a kind to be trusted in emergencies. In most cases, it is not "*skin* deep." Those who were Abolitionists in the teeth of popular opposition are the only ones who really made the case of the colored people their own; therefore they are the ones least likely to be hoodwinked by sophistry and false pretenses now.

To us the present crisis of the country seems more dangerous than that of '61. The insidiousness of oppressors is always more to be dreaded than their open violence. There can be no reasonable doubt that a murderous feeling toward the colored people prevails extensively at the South; and we are far from feeling very sure that a large party could not be rallied at the North in favor of restoring slavery. We have no idea that it ever *can* be restored; but if we avert the horrors of another war, more dreadful than the last, we must rouse up and keep awake a public sentiment that will compel politicians to do their duty. This we consider the appropriate and all-important work of the old Anti-slavery Society.

The British Anti-slavery Society deserted their post too soon. If they had been as watchful to protect the freed people of the West Indies as they were zealous to emancipate them, that horrid catastrophe in Jamaica might have been avoided. The state of things in those islands warns us how dangerous it is to trust those who have been slaveholders, and those who habitually sympathize with slaveholders, to frame laws and regulations for liberated slaves. As well might wolves be trusted to guard a sheepfold.

We thank God, friend Phillips, that you are preserved and strengthened to be a wakeful sentinel on the watch-tower, ever ready to be a wakeful nation against selfish, timid politicians, and dawdling legislators, who manifest no trust either in God or the people.

> Yours faithfully,
> David L. Child,
> L. Maria Child.

[Parton, pp. 63-64]

Proclamation of Thanksgiving Day

Although his early career as a soldier and farmer proved mostly desultory, Ulysses S. Grant (1822-1885) rose to a place of distinction and honor during the War Between the States (1861-1865). He began that war as a commissioned colonel and quickly rose to general in the first year of the conflict. From 1862-63 he commanded a succession of dazzling triumphs from Vicksburg to Chattanooga, and President Lincoln rewarded him with overall control of the Union war effort. It was to Grant that General Robert E. Lee surrendered in April 1865.

Three years later the general won the U.S. presidency as a Republican candidate, beginning a rather frustrating two terms in office in which his cabinet and political contributors sorely let him down. Grant went untouched by the scandals and corruption all around him. Nevertheless, he was out of his element as President.

He was unable to secure harmony and honor among his cabinet officials, but Grant was determined to promote those qualities among the states that had so recently warred with each other. In his first year in the Oval Office, Grant's proclamation to the American people of a Thanksgiving Day observation spoke of the unity and goodwill for which he yearned.

"I, Ulysses S. Grant, President of the United States, do recommend that Thursday, the 18th day of November next, be observed as a day of thanksgiving and of praise and of prayer to Almighty God. . . ."

October 5, 1869

The year which is drawing to a close has been free from pestilence; health has prevailed throughout the land; abundant crops reward the labors of the husbandman; commerce and manufactures have successfully prosecuted their peaceful paths; the mines and forests have yielded liberally; the nation has increased in wealth and in strength; peace has prevailed, and its blessings have advanced every interest of the people in every part of the Union; harmony and fraternal intercourse restored are obliterating the marks of past conflict and estrangement; burdens have been lightened; means have been increased; civil and religious liberty are secured to every inhabitant of the land, whose soil is trod by none but freemen.

It becomes a people thus favored to make acknowledgment to the Supreme Author from whom such blessings flow of their gratitude and their dependence, to render praise and thanksgiving for the same, and devoutly to implore a continuance of God's mercies.

Therefore I, Ulysses S. Grant, President of the United States, do recommend that Thursday, the 18th day of November next, be observed as a day of thanksgiving and of praise and of prayer to Almighty God, the creator and the ruler of all the people of the United States to accustomed places of public worship and to unite in the homage and praise due to the bountiful Father of All Mercies and in fervent prayer for the continuance of the manifold blessings he has vouchsafed to us as a people.

In testimony whereof I have hereunto set my hand and caused the seal of the United States to be affixed, this 5th day of October, A.D. (SEAL) 1869, and of the Independence of the United States of America the ninety-fourth.

U.S. Grant

[Moran, p. 24]

"Women of this day!"

In 1870, when the Franco-Prussian War broke out in Europe, the cherished American writer Julia Ward Howe (1819-1910) was disgusted and alarmed by the cruelty of the fighting. She couldn't understand why the conflict hadn't been decided by diplomacy rather than what she regarded as a barbaric waste of human life. After going through the Civil War and its sufferings, Howe wanted to do something to stop the bloodshed between nations. Then it occurred to her that as a woman and a mother, she could.

In 1870 she wrote an "Appeal to Womanhood Throughout the World," an open letter to her global sisters pleading with them to protect the lives of the children they had labored long and hard to bring into the world. The letter was translated into many languages, including French, Spanish, Italian, German and Swedish.

"The sword of murder is not the balance of justice! Blood does not wipe out dishonor nor violence indicate possession."

Arise, then, women of this day!

Arise all women who have hearts, whether your baptism be that of water or of fears!

Say firmly: "We will not have great questions decided by irrelevant agencies,

"Our husbands shall not come to us reeking with carnage, for caresses and applause,

"Our sons shall not be taken from us to unlearn all that we have been able to teach them of charity, mercy, and patience."

We women of one country will be too tender of those of another country to allow our sons to be trained to injure theirs.

From the bosom of the devastated earth a voice goes up with our own. It says, "Disarm, Disarm!"

The sword of murder is not the balance of justice! Blood does not wipe out dishonor nor violence indicate possession.

As men have often forsaken the plow and the anvil at the summons of war, let women now leave all that may be left of home for a great and earnest day of counsel.

Let them meet first, as women, to bewail and commemorate the dead.

Let them then solemnly take counsel with each other as the means whereby the great human family can live in peace,

And each bearing after her own time the sacred impress, not of Caesar, but of God.

[fcarpenter@mail.edgenet.net]

D.L. Moody: Evangelist and Family Man

Evangelist Dwight L. Moody (1837-1899) spent a great deal of time traveling to revival meetings throughout the United States and Great Britain, which meant extended periods away from his family. He kept in touch with them, however, through the mail, frequently scratching out hasty messages filled with tenderness and fatherly concern.

In the first letter printed here, he wishes his son Willie a happy fifteenth birthday and looks ahead to a bright future for the young man. The letter was written during Moody's two-year sojourn in England when he spoke to some two-and-a-half million people in the midst of an enormous revival in the British Isles.

"I send you much love & good wishes & may you live to take the place of your father in the blessed work of leading souls to Christ. . . ."

March 22/84

My dear Willie

By the time you get this note you will be 15 and I want to tell you how thankful I am that you have been spaird [sic] to us a nother [sic] year & I trust the new year before you will be your best year & that you will grow in all the graces Gal[atians] 5-22&23[.] I am earnestly praying that God may make you a useful man[.] I have a present for you but I am gone [sic] to keep it until you get here[.] it is like one I have for Ma Ma [one word unclear] pictures[.] Enclosed I also send you $5[.] I wanted to get you a nice present with the money but it is so hard to get any thing that you can take around with you as you travel about[.] I send you much love & good wishes & may you live to take the place of your father in the blessed work of leading souls to Christ is the prayer of your father[.]

D.L. Moody

[BGC Archives]

Moody's extensive travels became trying to him, especially when his daughter-in-law, Mary Whittle Moody, gave birth to his grandson, Dwight Lyman, on November 7, 1897. The preacher expressed his homesickness for her a little over a week later.

Fargo
Nov 17th 1897

My dear Mary

I have not writen thinking you would not be strong enough to read but I heard last night through my letters from home proved that you wer getting strong & I was very glad[.] I am in hopes that by the time you get this you will be able to get up[.] I have thought of you by day and dreamed of you by night[.] I was in hopes when I was at home it would have been all over or I should never have planned to have been away so far[.] it was a trying time for me & it must have been for your father[,] dear man. I do want to see you all & as soon as I can get a way from home I shall start[.] Kiss the newcomer for & dear little Irene tell her I am longing to see her

Hoping to be able to be you in December & see a good deal of you all[.]

> I am your homesick Father
> in law
> D.L. Moody
> [BGC Archives]

An American Philanthropist

Andrew Carnegie (1835-1919) was born in Scotland but made his lasting mark in America. He had just an elementary school education, but Carnegie valued books and ideas and social reforms. In 1848 the Carnegies moved to the United States, settling in Pittsburgh. Andrew worked on the Pennsylvania Railroad from 1853-1865. He then focused on his own businesses—the Keystone Bridge Company and his iron and steel works—both of which made him an exceptionally wealthy man.

Carnegie believed that even more important than making money was sharing one's blessings with others less fortunate. He also maintained that having great riches meant nothing if one was spiritually poor. The industrialist spent enormous sums of money building schools, libraries and museums to enrich the human spirit. He lived during a time in which many Americans adhered to the Christian teaching that the "haves" had a responsibility to take care of society's "have-nots." Carnegie maintained that to die wealthy would be a disgrace. At the time of his death, he had given away nearly $351 million.

When two Pittsburgh-area boroughs, Chartiers and Mansfield, consolidated, they chose the name "Carnegie" for their new town. Andrew and Mrs. Carnegie were so pleased by the gesture that they decided to build a library for their municipal namesake.

"I will spend $200,000 upon a fireproof building for a Public Library and a High School, also $10,000 to furnish the first supply of books."

26 April 1898

Dear Sirs,

I am glad to receive your communication of the 31st of March, proving as it does that the citizens of Carnegie are awake and interested in High Schools and Libraries. I will spend $200,000 upon a fireproof building for a Public Library and a High School, also $10,000 to furnish the first supply of books.

In this case the community will have to undertake to maintain the Library, but as they would get a High School for nothing I presume there would be no objection to this.

Or, say half the money can be used in building a Library. I would give another $100,000 in 5% gold bonds, which would furnish $5,000 a year to maintain the Library. In this case, however, the community would have to provide a High School for itself.

I find that a Public Hall in connection with a Library is of great moment. If you will visit the Library and Hall at Braddock's, Homestead, or at Pittsburg, and inquire, you will find that at Braddock's and Homestead especially the Hall is much used and greatly valued. Entertainments of all kinds, Amateur Performances, Meetings of Citizens, & are held in it. The receipts of the Hall at Pittsburg amount to quite a sum each year, and perhaps the Hall at Carnegie would yield a little revenue. Personally I would prefer this to uniting the High School to the Library, because public education is a thing apart, and it is a privilege for a community to pay for it.

It has been suggested to me that accommodation is needed for the Town Council in addition to the Hall and Library, or a building for High School and Library.

The whole matter is that there is a gift of $200,000 for Carnegie—Let us see the best use that can be made of it, except that there must be a Public Library and provision made for its maintenence.

> Very truly yours,
> Andrew Carnegie
> Messrs William Hill and
> George Hosack,
> Carnegie, Pa.
> [Internet Website, Andrew Carnegie Free Library]

7

Over There:
Letters of World War I and Later

W HEN THE ASSASSINATION of Austrian
Archduke Francis Ferdinand ignited the
First World War in the summer of 1914, it
took most Americans by surprise. By the
turn of the nineteenth century, many believed strongly that progress and reason,
aided by technology, would triumph over
the archaic, problem-solving method of
war. Indeed, the twentieth century was to
be the "Christian Century."

Rather than becoming better, however,
mankind devised new ways to engage in
barbaric cruelty, as evidenced by the Great
War, which it was initially called. Nations
mobilized their massive resources and
hurled them at each other murderously.
Machine guns made old-style frontal at-

tacks suicidal. Soldiers dug trenches for their protection against the modern weapons, but poison gas seeped its monstrous way into those furrows. World War I was not a matter of movement and attack, but of attrition. Man became the slave, not the master, of the weapons he had created.

By 1915 Russia had buried two-and-a-half million soldiers and twenty percent of its civilians. Six thousand Europeans died for every day of the war, and material losses soared astronomically. After the communist takeover of Russia in 1917, the U.S. entered the conflict, fearful that Europe stood on the precipice of complete destruction. As President Woodrow Wilson explained, "The world must be safe for democracy."

This period of destruction, and the era of disillusion that followed, are highlighted in the following letters.

TR Speaks to the Troops

Although Woodrow Wilson occupied the White House, millions of Americans still revered their beloved former President, Theodore Roosevelt (1858-1919), and looked to him for wisdom and inspiration, particularly during the war. He was a man who had known action in the battlefield himself, having led a volunteer cavalry unit known as the "Rough Riders" during the Spanish-American War (1898). He also would know the heartache of losing a son in the global conflict that opened the twentieth century.

The New York Bible Society appealed to former President Roosevelt, asking him to write a letter to the troops preparing to enter the conflict. That message appeared in all the New Testaments given to each American soldier heading "over there" to Europe's battlefields.

"The most perfect machinery of government will not keep us as a nation from destruction if there is not within us a soul. No abounding of material prosperity shall avail us if our spiritual senses atrophy."

The teaching of the New Testament is foreshadowed in Micah's verse, "What more doth the Lord require of thee than to do justice, and to *love mercy*, and to *walk humbly* with thy God." *Do justice;* and therefore fight valiantly against those that stand for the reign of Moloch and Beelzebub on this earth. *Love mercy*; treat your enemies well; succor the afflicted; treat every woman as if she were your sister; care for the little children; and be tender with the old and helpless. *Walk humbly*; you will do so if you study the life and teachings of the Savior, walking in His steps. And remember: the most perfect machinery of government will not keep us as a nation from destruction if there is not within us a soul. No abounding of material prosperity shall avail us if our spiritual senses atrophy. The foes of our own household will surely prevail against us unless there be in our people an inner life which gives its outward expression in a morality like unto that preached by the seers and prophets of God when the grandeur that was Greece and the glory that was Rome still lay in the future.

[Grant, p. 108]

The Spiritual Secret of a Hero

The strapping, winsome Tennessean Alvin C. York (1887-1964), was one of America's most celebrated heroes of World War I. York was born in Pall Mall to a blacksmithing and farming family that included seven other boys and three girls. They lived in a one-room cabin. York's education ended around the third grade, which wasn't unusual in that place and time.

Mr. and Mrs. York taught their third son what was most necessary in life—how to handle a plow, a rifle and a Bible. Nevertheless, Alvin strayed from the fold in his youth. When York realized that he was breaking his mother's heart and that he had no chance of winning the heart of his beloved Miss Gracie Williams the way he was, he gave up drinking, swearing, chewing and fighting. Another life change quickly followed. Under the influence of evangelist M.H. Russell, York became a Christian.

The young man had made his peace with his family, his girl and the Lord, but the world was not at peace. Alvin received a notice to register for the draft in June, 1917 while working on a state highway, one that, ironically, would come to be named for him. Although he reported to his local board, the twenty-nine-year-old struggled and prayed over the idea of killing men in a war. After an intense inner struggle, York concluded that in order to be a man of peace, he first had to help win this war.

Although his pastor tried to get him excused from armed service based on conscientious objection, York refused to sign the papers. He went on to become the hero of the Meuse-Argonne battle where, in the waning days of the war, he commanded a small detachment against a Ger-

man machine-gun emplacement. *With seventeen shots, York killed seventeen enemy soldiers. Then, out of bullets, he killed eight more with his pistol, prompting 132 Germans to surrender.*

Before he was awarded the Congressional Medal of Honor, before the glory days of his homecoming, then-Private Alvin York wrote one last letter to his Miss Gracie before leaving for France in the spring of 1918. Writing letters came with great difficulty for him, but he took the time for this painstaking effort knowing how much it would mean to her.

"I mean by the Grace of God to come back to you some day. And say darling, I am so glad to know that you have promised to be True to me until I come back."

Co. G 328th Inf.
Camp Upton, L.I.,
New York
April 23, 1918

411 2nd St.
Miss Gracie Williams

My Dearest Darling

I will try to write you a few lines to night as I have just got in camp and got my bed fixed and It is now a bout 930 o clock. Well say dear you know I wrote and told you a bout the other boys that started before we did. When we got here they were gone to France. They just left to day. So our major told us boys to night that we would go in a short time. So I want you to answer that other letter that I wrote you and answer them questions that I ask you to answer in regard to your slippers and dress. So please answer them all. And say, Miss Gracie please answer as soon as you get this letter for I want to hear from you once more before I sail, ho ho. For I love you. So I will only say I mean by the Grace of God to come back to you some day. And say darling, I am so glad to know that you have promised to be True to me until I come back. I sure will be true to you darling, and if I should never get back to you darling, you can say that your best Lover and your Truest Sweetheart is gone. But please remember if you meet me there you will have to git right with God.

I am longing to see you. But I will sail for france in a bout ten days I guess at the longest, and I sure want to hear from you before I go. For its you I love. Oh yes Gracie there is not a day nor a night but what you are on my mind. Oh I never had so great love for no one as I have for you.

Oh say darling we come through 11 states to get where we are. The boys is almost half drunk to night. We come across a lake area at Baltimore, Maryland and you couldn't see anything hardly but water. We come through Philadelphia City and New York City and Washington, D.C., Newark, N.J., and Richmond, Va. We come through the biggest citys of 11 states and we crossed two or three lakes. Well darling you are the girl I love as mine. Oh my darling if I just knowed what to do to pleasure you and make you happy until I get back to you. And darling you can—will you not love me in return? I feel that I shall be rewarded with a sweet kiss when next we meet. Don't you think so, ho ho. Well say darling now don't you think because you and I are not married that you wont take those slippers for it you mean to be mine when I come back you need not to care for I love you and I want to get you those things and now if you don't take them it will look like that you don't mean to marry me when I get back from France. But if I get killed you can say that I died that you might stay free. Oh say darling I wish that you and me had married when I was at home. Then I would have knowed that you would have been taken good care of and you would have plenty of money to have got you eney thing that you wanted. And say dear then if I never got back you would have got $10,000.00 Thousand Dollars and that would have done you as long as you live and then you could have eney thing you wanted. But the way it is I am worrying dear a bout you having to do the way you do. But oh say darling if I live to git back I sure want you to be mine to keep forever; and listen darling if I don't never git back will you go and stay with mother? That is my request, for Mother will have plenty of money and she sure will take care of you and you won't have to work, only just help Mother in the house. Oh say darling I can't never be satisfied as long as you are talking to the other boys so please promise me that you will not go with one while I am in france. Oh say darling, do you love me well enough to promise me that. I hope you do, for darling I love you so well that it almost breaks my heart to think of you going with some other one. Oh say darling don't go with any one will you not. Please don't. And dear if you love me please take good care of your self. Will you promise me that you will take good care of your self?

Please do for I love you. Darling, say in regard to those pictures, you write me when you answer this letter and tell me if she got them. Please answer soon as you get this letter with a long letter and please answer all my questions. So in regard to what you said a bout you told me the first time I left you in November you know where we were at and you told me just before I left you. Say you remember you were crying and I asked you not to let eney other boys kiss you and asked you to promise me that and you said you would not let eney one kiss you. So I hope you will hold your promise and be true.

So I will close. But you know darling its hard to say good-bye sweetheart. But just think that I am coming back if the Lord permits and I hope he will. So please answer soon as you git this letter for I sure want to hear from you once more. So I will write you darling if I go to france. So don't think I will forgit you. So good-bye from your loving sweetheart, with a kiss.

Alvin C. York

[Perry, pp. 75-77]

Taking a Stand against Skepticism

The Great War, having dashed the optimism with which the new century began, was followed by a period of skepticism. In the 1920s the theory of evolution as an explanation for the existence of life posed a serious threat to the Christian faith. Particularly in the public sphere academics and scientists abandoned the faith of America's fathers and mothers in favor of a shaky hypothesis that never has been proven.

One scientist who refused to compromise or dismiss his belief that the God of Abraham, Isaac and Jacob created the universe and everything in it was George Washington Carver (c. 1864-1943). A son of former slaves, Carver earned a bachelor's degree around the age of thirty. He then became the first black American to distinguish himself in the international scientific arena through his work. The Missouri-born man served as the director of agricultural research at Tuskegee Institute in Alabama, a post he held for nearly fifty years.

Carver saw no conflict whatsoever between science and religion. He once told a friend, "I am not interested in science or any thing else that leaves God out of it" [National Park Service]. In the spring of 1925 Carver wrote to a Seattle minister about the verity of the Bible's account of creation.

"I am fearful lest our finite research will be wholly unable to grasp the infinite details of creation, and therefore we lose the great truth of the creation of man."

March 24, 1925

My dear Rev. Kunzman:

Thank you for your good letter. . . .

Now as to your questions, I regret that I cannot be of much service to you as I have not devoted much time to such investigations in proportion to the almost life time researches of some.

I am interested of course, intensely interested. My life time study of nature in it's many phazes leads me to believe more strongly than ever in the Biblical account of man's creation as found in Gen.1:27 "And God created man in his own image, in the image of God created He him; male and female created he them."

Of course sciences through all of the ages have been searching for the so called "missing link" which enables us to interpret man from his very beginning, up to his present high state of civilization.

I am fearful lest our finite research will be wholly unable to grasp the infinite details of creation, and therefore we lose the great truth of the creation of man.

Yours very truly,
Geo. W. Carver
[National Park Service]

Carver's Conversion

Illiterate until the age of twenty, George Washington Carver went on to earn both bachelor's and master's de-

grees from Iowa State College. He became one of America's leading agricultural scientists, using empirical methods to discover diverse uses for common products. His goal was to train black farmers in agriculture and home economics. Carver's discovery of hundreds of commodities derived from peanuts, soybeans and sweet potatoes led the South away from a single-crop system to a more diversified agriculture.

At the heart of Carver's work was his faith in Jesus Christ. In this letter to a Greensboro, North Carolina writer who wanted to include him in a book she was doing, the great scientist recounted his own conversion.

July 24, 1931

My dear Miss Coleman:

Thank you very much for your splendid letter. I thoroughly believe you can get a much better subject to go in your book than myself. After thinking it over again, searching around, if you still feel that I ought to go in there, you have my permission.

The facts in "Upward Climb" are correct, as the writer came here and got the story.

As to being a Christian, please write to Mr. Hardwick, Y.M.C.A., 706 Standard Building, Atlanta, Georgia. The dear boy made a ten days tour with me through Virginia, North Carolina, and Tennessee, where I lectured to a number of colleges and universities. We came together in prayer often to get our spiritual strength renewed. Whenever we come into a great project, we meet and ask God's guidance. Mr. Hardwick will tell you things that I could not. We both believe in Divine guidance.

Prov. 3:6; Phil. 4:13; Psalms 119:18; these are our slogan passages.

I was just a mere boy when converted, hardly ten years old. There isn't much of a story to it. God just came into my heart one afternoon while I was alone in the "loft" of our big barn while I was shelling corn to carry to the mill to be ground into meal.

A dear little white boy, one of our neighbors, about my age came by one Saturday morning and in talking and playing he told me he was going to Sunday school tomorrow morning. I was eager to know what a Sunday school was. He said they sang hymns and prayed. I asked him what prayer was and what they said. I do not remember what he said; only remember that as soon as he left I climbed up into the "loft", knelt down by the barrel of corn and prayed as best I could. I do not remember what I said. I only recall that I felt so good that I prayed several times before I quit.

My brother and myself were the only colored children in that neighborhood and of course, we could not go to church or Sunday school, or school of any kind.

That was my simple conversion, and I have tried to keep the faith.

Games were very simple in my boyhood days in the country. Baseball, running, jumping, swimming, and checkers constituted the principal ones. I played all of them.

My favorite song was "Must Jesus Bear the Cross Alone and all the world go free, etc."

If I had leisure time from roaming the woods and fields, I put it in knitting, crocheting, and other forms of fance (sic) work.

I am sending you, under separate cover some literature which may be of service.

Very sincerely yours,
G.W. Carver, Director

[National Park Service]

Science and Divine Inspiration

One of George Washington Carver's goals was to unify science and religion. In a November 1924 speech at New York's Marble Collegiate Church he asserted that his success as a scientist was because God had revealed knowledge in various forms to him. A case in point was the many uses for the peanut that Carver had discovered. He told the church audience, "I never have to grope for methods: the method is revealed at the moment I am inspired to create something new" [Kremer, p. 128].

An editorial appeared in the New York Times *two days later attacking Carver's position, charging that the black scientist completely lacked a true scientific spirit. The pioneering Carver responded in a letter of his own.*

November 24, 1924

My dear Sir:

I have read with much interest your editorial pertaining to myself in the issue of November 20th.

I regret exceedingly that such a gross misunderstanding should arise as to what was meant by "Divine inspiration." Inspiration is never at variance with information; in fact, the more information one has, the greater will be the inspiration.

Paul, the great Scholar, says, Second Timothy 2-15, "Study to show thyself approved unto God, a Workman that needeth not to be ashamed, rightly dividing the word of truth."

Again he says in Galatians 1-12, "For I neither received it of man, neither was I taught it, but by the revelation of Jesus Christ."

Many, many other equally strong passages could be cited, but these two are sufficient to form a base around which to cluster my remarks. In the first verse, I have followed and am yet following the first word of study.

I am a graduate of the Iowa State College of Agriculture and Mechanical Arts, located at Ames, Iowa, taking two degrees in Scientific Agriculture. Did considerable work in Simpson College, Indianola, along the lines of Art, Literature and Music. . . .

I receive the leading scientific publications. I thoroughly understand that there are scientists to whom the world is merely the result of chemical forces or material electrons. I do not belong to this class. I fully agree with the Rt. Rev. Irving Peake Johnson, D.D., bishop of Colorado in a little pamphlet entitled "Religion and the Supernatural." It is published and distributed by the Trinity Parish of your own city. I defy any one who has an open mind to read this leaflet through and then deny there is such a thing as Divine inspiration.

In evolving new creations, I am wondering of what value a book would be to the creator if he is not a master of analytical work, both qualitative and quantitative. I can see readily his need for the book from which to get his analytical methods. The master analyst needs no book; he is at liberty to take apart and put together substances, compatible or non compatible to suit his own particular taste or fancy.

While in your beautiful city, I was struck with the large number of Taros and Yautias displayed in many of your markets; they are edible roots imported to this country largely from Trinidad, Porto Rico, China, Dutch Guina, and Peru. Just as soon as I saw these luscious roots, I marveled at the wonderful possibilities for their expansion. Dozens of things came to me while standing there looking at them. I should follow the same or similar lines I have pursued in developing products from the white potato. I know of no one who has ever worked with these roots in this way. I know of no book from which I can get this information, yet I will have no trouble in doing it.

If this is not inspiration and information from a source greater than myself, or greater than any one has wrought up to the present time, kindly tell me what it is.

"And ye shall know the truth and the truth shall make you free." John 8-32.

Science is simply the truth about anything.

Yours very truly,
Geo. W. Carver

[National Park Service]

The Glory of God in Nature

Carver regarded the natural world as a laboratory for discovering more about the Creator God. To him, the earth was God's workshop. He once said, "nature in its varied forms are the little windows through which God permits me to commune with Him, and to see much of His glory, majesty, and power by simply lifting the curtain and looking in" [Kremer, p. 143].

In a letter to a friend, a Denver, Colorado YMCA official, Carver expressed his desire that young people would get to know and better understand God by studying nature.

March 1, 1927

My beloved Friend, Mr. Boyd:

How good of you to write me, and such a wonderful letter it is. . . . One of the most beautiful, hopeful, and encouraging things of growing interest, is that there is springing up here and there groups of college bred young men and women, who are willing to know us by permitting themselves to get acquainted with us.

The two little snaps are so beautiful, naturally, God has been so lavish in the display of His handiwork. It is indeed so much more impressive however when you feel that God met with that fine body of students.

My dear friend, I am so glad that God is using you in such an efficient way.

My beloved friend, I do not feel capable of writing a single word of counsel to those dear young people, more than to say that my heart goes out to every one of them, regardless of the fact that I have never seen them and may never do so.

O how I want them to get the fullest measure of happiness and success out of life. I want them to see the Great Creator in the smallest and apparently the most insignificant things about them.

How I long for each one to walk and talk with him. Just last week I was reminded of His omnipotence, majesty and power through a little specimen of mineral sent me for analysis, from Bakersfield, California. I have dissolved it, purified it, made conditions favorable for the formation of crystals, when lo before my very eyes, a beautiful bunch of sea green crystals have formed and alongside of them a bunch of snow white ones.

Marvel of marvels, how I wish I had you in God's little workshop for a while, how your soul would be thrilled and lifted up.

My beloved friend, keep your hands in that of the Master, walk daily by His side, so that you may lead others into the realms of true happiness, where a religion of hate, (which poisons both body and soul) will be unknown, having in its place the "Golden Rule" way, which is the "Jesus Way" of life, will reign supreme. Then, we can walk and talk with Jesus momentarily, because we will be attuned to His will and wishes, thus making the Creation story of the world non-debateable as to its reality.

God, my beloved friend is infinite the highest embodiment of love. We are finite, surrounded and often filled with hate.

We can only understand the infinite as we loose the finite and take on the infinite.

My dear friend, my friendship to you cannot possibly mean what yours does to me. I talk to God through you, you help me see God through another angle. . . .

Most sincerely yours
G.W. Carver

[National Park Service]

Spiritual Truth from Botanical Study

Carver had special relationships with a group of young men whom he encouraged as a spiritual and scientific father. Among the dearest of those was a Virginian named Jimmie Hardwick. As his mentor, Carver wrote to Hardwick frequently, encouraging the young man to find God in his study of nature. In a 1932 letter he also illustrated how God used a lesson in botany to teach him a great life principle, that when God closes one door, it is often in order to open a far better one.

July 1, 1932

My Beloved Spiritual Boy, Mr. Hardwick:

Dear, I must tell you about an experience I had today, which shows so clearly that God moves in a mysterious way His wonders to perform.

Before we left for Miss. while dear Howard was here the first time, I made some collections of fungi some distance away. Occasionally my mind would urge me to go back there again. The urge became so strong this morning that I went. I found the place grown up with weeds and briars.

I began pulling the dead limbs out but the wasps had built a nest in it and soon ran me away without stinging me. I stood afar off quite perplexed, started home, proceeded a little ways and spied another pile of brush. I went to it and found it to be one of the richest finds that I had yet made.

God closed the first door that I might see one open with greater opportunities. This is often so when we are sorely disappointed in some of our fondest dreams.

You have seemed to be with me all day today. May God ever be with my great spiritual boy, my pioneer boy, my oldest boy, in fact God's pioneer boy.

> With so much love and
> admiration,
> G.W. Carver
> [National Park Service]

8

Hope and Opportunity:
Letters of World War II and Later

MANY WARS HAVE punctuated American history with the roar of canons and the moans of the dying and their loved ones. The Revolution, War of 1812, Civil War, Spanish-American War, World Wars I and II, Korea, Vietnam, and the Gulf War all brought their share both of glory and misery in our nation's attempt to secure and protect its people's freedoms. The following letters from World War II and its aftermath demonstrate how faith in God sustained those at the front as well as the ones who waited for them at home.

Hope in God's Deliverance

As Prime Minister Winston Churchill (1874-1965) steadied the British ship of state during the trying years of World War II (1939-1945), he maintained a lively correspondence with President Franklin D. Roosevelt. On June 10, 1940, in the midst of the turbulent Battle of Britain, Churchill wrote to FDR after listening to the President's radio speech dealing with Italy's attack on France. In Churchill's words, the message was "magnificent . . . instinct with passion and carrying to us the message of hope."

Hope in God's deliverance from Nazi tyranny kept Churchill strong in those days. Before retiring that night, he wrote to Roosevelt, identifying himself with a phrase he often used in their personal correspondence: "Former Naval Person."

"Your statement that the material aid of the United States will be given to the Allies in their struggle is a strong encouragement in a dark but not unhopeful hour."

Former Naval Person to President Roosevelt.

We all listened to you last night and were fortified by the good scope of your declaration. Your statement that the material aid of the United States will be given to the Allies in their struggle is a strong encouragement in a dark but not unhopeful hour. Everything must be done to keep France in the fight and to prevent any idea of the fall of Paris, should it occur, becoming the occasion of any king of parley. The hope with which you inspire them may give them the strength to persevere. They should continue to defend every yard of their soil and use the full fighting force of their Army. Hitler, thus baffled of quick results, will turn upon us, and we are preparing ourselves to resist his fury and defend our island. Having saved the B.E.F. [British Expeditionary Force], we do not lack troops at home, and as soon as divisions can be equipped on the much higher scale needed for Continental service they will be despatched to France. Our intention is to have a strong army fighting in France for the campaign of 1941. I have already cabled you about aeroplanes, including flying-boats, which are so needful to us in the impending struggle for the life of Great Britain. But even more pressing for us is the need for destroyers. The Italian outrage makes it necessary for us to cope with a much larger number of submarines which may come out into the Atlantic and perhaps be based on Spanish ports. To this the only counter is destroyers. Nothing is so important as for us to have the thirty or forty old destroyers you have already had reconditioned. We can fit them very rapidly with our Asdics, and they will bridge the gap of six months before our wartime new construction comes into play. We will return them or their equivalent to you, without fail, at six months' notice if at any time you need them. The next six months are vital. If while we have to guard the East Coast against invasion a new heavy German-Italian submarine attack is launched against our commerce, the strain may be beyond our resources, and the ocean traffic by which we live may be strangled. Not a day should be lost. I send you my heartfelt thanks and those of my colleagues for all you are doing and seeking to do for what we may now, indeed, call the Common Cause.

[Churchill, pp. 114-115]

Supporting the Troops

George C. Marshall (1880-1959) first distinguished himself during World War I while astutely organizing the transfer of troops in the Meuse-Argonne operation. As a result he became General John Pershing's chief aide. An able administrator, Marshall developed the Civilian Conservation Corps in the 1930's and then played a pivotal role in training the American army to fight World War II.

Although Winston Churchill described him as "the true organizer" of the Allied victory in World War II, General Marshall realized that at the core of our nation's efforts to preserve, protect and defend its liberties, stood the Christian faith. We get an inkling of this from a letter he wrote to his rector, J. Manly Cobb, of Leesburg, Virginia during the summer of 1944.

"It is reassuring to know that the churches are maintaining contact with their soldiers which . . . is very helpful to morale."

August 17, 1944

My dear Cobb:

I shall be much pleased to be represented by a star on the Service Flag of St. James Church, and appreciate your having me so in mind.

Thank you for the prayer book and cross which accompanied your note. It is reassuring to know that the churches are maintaining contact with their soldiers in this manner, which, aside from the benefits to the individual, is very helpful to morale.

> With my regards,
> Faithfully yours,
> George C. Marshall

[George C. Marshall Collection]

General Douglas MacArthur: Christianity and a Nation's Character

At the conclusion of the war, General Douglas MacArthur commanded the occupation army in Japan, helping that nation rebuild on more democratic principles. During this time the five-star general answered with alacrity a request from Dr. Louie D. Newton, President of the Southern Baptist Convention in Atlanta, Georgia. The clergyman wanted to know MacArthur's sentiments regarding the role of Christianity in a nation's character.

He also responded to a similar question put forth in another letter by the Rev. James Flint Boughton of the Wesley Methodist Church of Pleasantville, New Jersey.

". . . there now exists an opportunity without counterpart since the birth of Christ for the spread of Christianity among the people of the Far East."

29 November, 1946

Dear Dr. Newton:

I am deeply grateful for your kind and thoughtful note of November 16th, and find both comfort and inspiration in the sentiments you express in behalf of that fine group of my fellow Americans who compose your convention.

The occupation of Japan from it[s] inception has proceeded with minimum display of Allied force. While its course has been firmly charted toward the achievement of our political objectives, progress has rested more upon the application of those guiding tenets of our Christian faith—justice, tolerance, understanding—which, without yielding firmness, have underwritten all applied policy, than upon the power or threat of Allied bayonets. This has deeply stirred the consciousness of the Japanese people and will have a far reaching and lasting influence upon the future of Japanese society. It has led them increasingly to turn to Christianity to strengthen realization of the complete failure of their own past and faith.

Due to the vacuum which events have left in the spiritual phase of Japanese life, there now exists an opportunity without counterpart since the birth of Christ for the spread of Christianity among the people of the Far East. If this opportunity is fully availed of by the leaders of our Christian faith, a revolution of the spirit may be expected to ensure which will more favorably alter the course of civilization than has any economic or political revolution accomplished in the history of the world. I know that you join me in the hope that we may rise to this opportunity and squarely meet its challenge.

> Faithfully yours,
> Douglas MacArthur
> [Gen. Douglas MacArthur Foundation]

Hope and Opportunity

22 November, 1947

Dear Dr. Boughton:

I am just in receipt of your fine letter of November 14th. . . .

It is gratifying to note your understanding of the need to emphasize with clarity the essential usefulness of Christianity in human progress. Democracy and Christianity have much in common, as practice of the former is impossible without giving faithful [word missing] to the fundamental concepts underlying the latter. In fact, it well may be that in the progress of mankind toward embracing Christianity, a devotion to these concepts in their political, social and spiritual sense may long precede their adoption with finality in a strictly religious sense—that peoples may learn to live by the tenets of Christianity and to cherish the way of life drawn from its dogmas, while yet following the ritual of another faith built upon divergent and irreconcilable historical teachings. It would seem essential, therefore, that theological knowledge be reduced insofar as possible to its practical application to existing realities, in order that assault upon tradition and superstition which oft' times buttresses the human mind against enlightened knowledge may be preceded by progressive absorption of the every day blessings to which our Christian faith give rise. This I am sure dominates your thinking and guides your approach to this great human problem.

Faithfully yours,
Douglas MacArthur.

[Gen. Douglas MacArthur Foundation]

MacArthur and the Bible

One of only six five-star generals in United States history, Douglas MacArthur was born in an army barracks in 1880 and died eighty-four years later at the Walter Reed Army Hospital. His long and distinguished career encompassed both world wars. He became a legendary figure during the latter conflict as Supreme Allied Commander of forces in the Southwest Pacific. In 1942, as he retreated from the Philippines to set up his headquarters on the Bataan Peninsula, MacArthur uttered his celebrated promise, "I shall return." In October, 1944, when the Americans landed on Leyte he proclaimed, "I have returned. By the grace of Almighty God, our forces stand again on Philippine soil" [Bartlett, p. 642]. When the Japanese surrendered in August, 1945, he took command of the occupational forces there.

Another famous episode in his life came when, during the Korean War, MacArthur was relieved of his duties in the Far East by President Harry Truman. In a joint meeting of Congress he said, "old soldiers never die; they just fade away. I now close my military career and just fade away" [Bartlett, p. 642].

People often requested that General MacArthur share his thoughts with them about the Christian faith. During the occupation of Japan, MacArthur responded to Mr. George T.B. Davis' request to describe his belief in the Bible and the blessings that it had brought to MacArthur over the years. An additional letter follows in which the general made a statement to the Pocket Testament League about the Bible's importance.

25 February 1948.

Dear Mr. Davis:

No greater force has contributed to American life and progress than the Holy Bible. for to it since the birth of our Republic American mothers have turned for inspiration, guidance and instruction in the early training of the young, and with the advent and departure of each successive generation its immutable concepts have fashioned the purpose and resteeled the will to advance the cause of human progress. All of our great leaders, from Washington on, solemnly have dedicated themselves to preserve, support and defend our Constitution, impregnable bulwark of our liberties, with hand upon this holy book, and thereafter never failed to find in it strength to meet the ensuing responsibilities of public duty.

Douglas MacArthur

[Gen. Douglas MacArthur Foundation]

4 April 1949

It gives me great pleasure to commend the reading of the Bible, God's immortal gift to the human race, for in its pages there is revealed that righteousness which exalteth a nation. In the Sacred Scriptures you will find the Saviour of the world Who is the chief cornerstone of all liberty, the basis of fair and honest government, and the foundation for a true and living faith in God Whose promises never fail.

Douglas MacArthur

[Gen. Douglas MacArthur Foundation]

Great Letters in American History

The Importance of Christian Education

Following the Allied victories in World War II, General MacArthur took a keen interest in educating German and Japanese children about democracy and its dependence on the Judeo-Christian ethic. During that time, George H. Davis of the Gospel Publishing House in Springfield, Missouri requested that General MacArthur write him with a statement about the religious education of American children to be used in The Superintendent's Assistant. *The General responded from his headquarters with the occupation army in Tokyo.*

Tokyo, Japan
30 June 1949

Dear Mr. Davis:

Replying to your note of June 23rd, I feel that the basic cause for the present world dislocation and unrest lies in the great disparity between the moral development and scientific advance of mankind. This gap may only be bridged by an awakening of the human race to its deficiency in spiritual values, as a prerequisite to accelerated moral progress. Apart from training in the American home, which is the keystone to the arch of our social development, the main hope for this awakening lies in the religious instruction of American youth in the Sunday Schools throughout the land. Upon those who have dedicated their time to such instruction, there thus rests the heavy burden of insuring that American youth of the present receive adequate spiritual

Hope and Opportunity

preparation to meet the challenging responsibility
of American leadership of the future.

Faithfully yours,
Douglas MacArthur

[Gen. Douglas MacArthur Foundation]

9

A Search for Truth:
Letters of the late Twentieth Century

Fʀᴏᴍ ᴛʜᴇ ᴄᴏʟᴅ-ᴡᴀʀ '50s through the politically charged '60s, the transitional '70s, the conservative '80s and the millennium-haunted '90s, one theme that has pervaded the American landscape is the search for truth, meaning and purpose. While the latter half of the twentieth century has seen everything from Christian revivals to the popular acceptance of New-Age beliefs, our culture is entering the new millennium without a moral consensus. Throughout this era, however, there have been many who have upheld Judeo- Christian values and those who have boldly shared their faith. The following letters reveal their stories.

A Scholar's Spiritual Search

While studying abroad at Oxford, American scholar Sheldon Vanauken and his wife, Jean "Davy" Davis, began searching the truth claims of Christianity. Their search was profoundly influenced by the writings of Professor C.S. Lewis. Van and Davy determined that if the deeply scholarly Lewis could believe that Jesus was, in fact, God, then Christianity deserved to be examined thoroughly. On an impulse Vanauken wrote to Lewis, who patiently answered many of the young scholar's questions and concerns. Vanauken did indeed go on to take the step of faith, joyfully sharing his decision with his mentor. The letters that follow, written during the winter of 1950-51, partially tell Vanauken's story of his faith journey.

"I have come to awareness of the strength and 'possibleness' of the Christian answer. I should like to believe it. I want to know God—if he is knowable."

To C.S. Lewis:

I write on an impulse—which in the morning may appear so immodest and presumptuous that I shall destroy this. But a few moments ago I felt that I was embarked for a voyage that would someday lead me to God. Even now, five minutes later, I'm inclined to add a qualifying "maybe". There is a leap I cannot make; it occurs to me that you, having made it, having linked certainty with Christianity, might not do it for me, but might give me a hint of how it's to be done. Having felt the aesthetic and historical appeal of Christianity, having begun to study it, I have come to awareness of the strength and "possibleness" of the Christian answer. I should like to believe it. I want to know God—if he is knowable. But I cannot pray with any conviction that Someone hears. I can't believe.

Very simply, it seems to me that some intelligent power made this universe and that all men must know it, axiomatically, and must feel awe at the power's infiniteness. It seems to me natural that men, knowing feeling so, should attempt to elaborate on that simplicity—the prophets, the Prince Buddha, the Lord Jesus, Mohammed, the Brahmins—and so arose the world's religions. But how can just one of them be singled out as true? To an intelligent visitor from Mars, would not Christianity appear to be merely one of a host of religions?

I said at starting that I felt I was treading a long road that would one day lead me to Christianity; I must, then, believe after a fashion that it is the truth. Or is it only that I want to believe it? But at the same time, something else in me says: "Wanting to believe is the way to self-deception. Honesty is better than any easy comfort. Have the courage to face the fact that all men may be nothing to the Power that made the suns."

And yet I would like to believe that the Lord Jesus is in truth my merciful God. For the apostles who could talk to Jesus, it must have been easy. But I live in a "real world" of red buses and nylon stockings and atomic bombs; I have only the record of others' claimed experiences with deity. No angels, no voices, nothing. Or, yes, one thing: living Christians. Somehow you, in this very same world, with the same data as I, are more meaningful to me than the bishops of the faithful past. You accomplished the leap from agnosticism to faith: how? I don't quite know how I dare write this to you, a busy Oxford don, not a priest. Yet I do know: you serve God, not yourself; you must do, if you're a Christian. Perhaps, if I had the wit to see it, my answer lies in the fact that I did write.

Sheldon Vanauken

Dear Mr. Vanauken:

My own position at the threshold of Xtianity was exactly the opposite of yours. You wish it were true; I strongly hoped it was not. At least, that was my conscious wish: you may suspect that I had unconscious wishes of quite a different sort and that it was these which finally shoved me in. True: but then I may equally suspect that under your conscious wish that it were true, there lurks a strong unconscious wish that it were not. What this works out to is that all that modern stuff about concealed wishes and wishful thinking, however useful it may be for explaining the origin of an error which you already know to be an error, is perfectly useless in deciding which of two beliefs is the error and which is the truth. For (a.) One never knows all one's wishes, and (b.) In very big questions, such as this, even one's conscious wishes are nearly always engaged on both sides. What I think one can say with certainty is this: the notion that everyone would like Xtianity to be true, and that therefore all atheists are brave men who have accepted the defeat of all their deepest desires, is simply impudent nonsense. Do you think people like Stalin, Hitler, Haldane, Stapledon (a corking good writer, by the way) wd. be pleased on waking up one morning to find that they were not their own masters, that they had a Master and a Judge, that there was nothing even in the deepest recesses of their thoughts about which they cd. say to Him "Keep out! Private. This is my business"? Do you? Rats! Their first reaction wd. be (as mine was) rage and terror. And I v. much doubt whether even you wd. find it simply pleasant. Isn't the truth this: that it wd. gratify some of our desires (ones we feel in fact pretty seldom) and outrage a great many others? So let's wash out all the wish business. It never helped anyone to solve any problem yet.

I don't agree with your picture of the history of religion—Christ, Buddha, Mohammed and others elaborating an original simplicity. I believe Buddhism to be a simplification of Hinduism and Islam to be a simplification of Xtianity. Clear, lucid, transparent, simple religion (Tao plus a shadowy, ethical god in the background) is a late development, usually arising among highly educated people in great cities. What you really start with is ritual, myth, and mystery, the death & return of Balder or Osiris, the dances, the initiations, the sacrifices, the divine kings. Over against that are the Philosophers, Aristotle or Confucius, hardly religious at all. The only two systems in which the mysteries and the philosophies come together are Hinduism & Xtianity: there you get both Metaphysics and Cult (continuous with the primeval cults). That is why my first step was to be sure that one or other of these had the answer. For the reality can't be one that appeals either only to savages or only to high brows. Real things aren't like that (e.g. matter is the first most obvious thing you meet—milk, chocolates, apples, and also the object of quantum physics.) There is no question of just a crowd of disconnected religions. The choice is between (a.) The materialist world picture: wh. I can't believe. b.) The real archaic primitive religions: wh. are not moral enough. (c.) The (claimed) fulfillment of these in Hinduism. (d.) The claimed fulfillment of these in Xtianity. But the weakness of Hinduism is that it doesn't really join the two strands. Unredeemably savage religion goes on in the village; the Hermit philosophises in the forest: and neither really interferes with the other. It is only Xtianity wh. compels a high brow like me to partake in a ritual blood feast, and also compels a central African convert to attempt an enlightened universal code of ethics. . . .

I don't know if any of this is the least use. Be sure to write again, or call, if you think I can be of any help.

Yours,
C.S. Lewis
[Vanauken, pp. 87-90]

The Search Continues

Over a period of months, Vanauken and Lewis continued their correspondence, with the former asking further, more penetrating questions about Christianity and religion. According to the young man, "My fundamental dilemma is this: I can't believe in Christ unless I have faith, but I can't have faith unless I believe in Christ" [Vanauken, p. 90]. At the end of Lewis' letter in response to the searching Vanauken, he said something that shocked the young man: "But I think you are already in the meshes of the net! The Holy Spirit is after you. I doubt if you'll get away!" Vanauken wrote of that time, "Alarm bells sounded, but I couldn't decide where to run" [p. 93]. At least, he commented, Christianity seemed exciting, both intellectually and aesthetically, and "The personality of Jesus emerged from the Gospels with astonishing consistency" [p. 93].

Davy Vanauken, deeply affected by C.S. Lewis' apologetical letters and books, as well as her mother's death, took the "leap" of faith first. Her husband held back for a few months, feeling a need for proof that Jesus was the risen Christ. Then the realization hit him that he couldn't go back to his "old easy-going theism" after all he had learned about Jesus. The only choices that remained either were to accept or reject the Lord. He finally concluded:

There might be no certainty that Christ was God—but, by God, there was no certainty that He was not. If I were to accept, I might and probably would face the thought through the years: "Perhaps, after all, it's a lie; I've been had!" But if I were to reject, I would certainly face the haunting, terrible thought: "Perhaps it's true—and I have *rejected* my God!" This was not to be borne. I *could not* reject Jesus.

[Vanauken, p. 98]

The Choice Is Made

One damp morning he wrote to C.S. Lewis.

I *choose* to believe in the Father, Son, and Holy Ghost—in Christ, my lord and my God. Christianity has the ring, the *feel*, of unique truth. Of *essential* truth. By it, life is made full instead of empty, meaningful instead of meaningless. Cosmos becomes beautiful at the *Centre*, instead of chillingly ugly beneath the lovely pathos of spring. But the emptiness, the meaninglessness, and the ugliness can only be seen, I think, when one has glimpsed the fullness, the meaning, and the beauty. It is when heaven and hell have *both* been glimpsed that going back is impossible. But to go on seemed impossible, also. A glimpse is not a vision. A choice was necessary: and there is no certainty. One can only choose a side. So I—I now choose my side: I choose beauty; I choose what I love. But choosing to believe *is* believing. It's all I can do: choose. I confess my doubts and ask my Lord Christ to enter my life. I do not *know* God is, I do but say: Be it unto me according to Thy will. I do not affirm that I am without doubt, I do but ask for help, having chosen, to overcome it. I do but say: Lord, I believe—help Thou mine unbelief.

[Vanauken, p. 99]

Unexpected Success

After the death of Senate Chaplain Peter Marshall in 1949, his widow Catherine (1914-1983) compiled his most popular sermons into a book called Mr. Jones, Meet the Master. *The public's enthusiastic response overwhelmed the publishing house—not to mention Marshall's widow. She went on to write his biography,* A Man Called Peter. *In the years since its release in 1951, the book has sold over four million copies.*

Catherine Marshall received thousands of letters from people who were touched by her books and Peter's special relationship with the Lord. Here are just a few:

"I thank God that I have lived to come face to face with the Master through Dr. Marshall's living words. . . ."

My dear Mrs. Marshall:

On my eighty-second birthday I was given a copy of *Mr. Jones, Meet the Master.* For almost seventy years I have been a church member. Yet Christianity as Dr. Marshall preached and lived it was unknown to me.

By the time I had finished the book my soul was flooded by a downpour of revelation. . . . I thank God that I have lived to come face to face with the Master through Dr. Marshall's living words. . . .

Dear Mrs. Marshall:

I have just finished reading *Mr. Jones, Meet the Master*. This comes to you to thank you from the depths of my heart for publishing this book. . . . From the opening word the book has been hard to put down. . . . For sheer beauty of language . . . the book is unsurpassed. . . . But far beyond that, its real value lies in its amazing ability to bring my Lord into my own living room. . . .

One letter even came from as far away as Nagasaki, Japan:

Dear Mrs. Marshall:

I've just finished your book *A Man Called Peter*. First I started to read it with a dictionary in hand around Christmas. Then I forgot I was reading in a foreign language and stopped looking up words. There existed no longer the barrier of language. I was happy with you, I was desperate with you. I have sobbed and cried with you, and now I am filled with the same bliss and gratefulness and happy memory that you are. . . .

What a dearest friend of us, Peter Marshall! The impact of him will not let me go again to despair or hatred of other men and myself. I found in him a fellow-Christian who really understands the daily presence of God in our common life, a G.G.P. (great-game-player) who encourages and understand my enthusiasm to Volley Ball, table tennis, Japanese chess, and photography. . . .

An Actor's Response

When A Man Called Peter *was made into a motion picture, Mrs. Marshall wrote to the actor chosen to portray Dr. Marshall, and was pleased to receive a reply.*

> Pinkneys Green
> Maidenhead
> Berks.

My dear Mrs. Marshall:

I was very pleased and very touched by your letter, and indeed by your kind thought in writing to me at all. . . .

I feel great humility and diffidence about my choice for this role. I am still very conscious of the fact that in appearance I cannot be as close as I would wish to the ideal person to personify Peter Marshall. . . .

I look forward very much indeed to meeting you while I am in America. . . . In the meantime, I would appreciate very much indeed any pointers which you could give me to help me with my characterisation. If you have any other recordings, might I borrow them from you for a time during the initial part of the progress on the film. . . .

In the meantime, again very many thanks for your kindness, and my sincere hope that our film will match up to the excellence of your book and to your memories.

Yours sincerely,
Richard Todd

[Marshall, pp. 15, 96-97, 178, 259-60]

The General with a Heart

Following World War II, General George C. Marshall organized the European recovery process, an effort that history remembers as the Marshall Plan. For his efforts he received the Nobel Peace Prize in 1953, the only professional soldier to be so awarded. In public appearances and in private letters he often spoke of the Christian principles necessary for the world to live at peace. On March 11, 1948, at the National Cathedral in Washington, Marshall said:

"Our greatest consolation has been in the love of those whom God has permitted to remain close to us and in the knowledge that His will is always wise and just."

The appeal to prayer has a powerful influence in American life because we are at heart a deeply religious people, though we do not always admit to it. . . . Prayer is one of the means of keeping alive our belief in the ultimate triumph of the Christian principles which underlie our civilization. This faith in our ideals is particularly important when we are forced to be realistic in face of an extremely serious world situation.

[George C. Marshall Collection,
Speeches and statements]

He knew firsthand the heartache and tragedies of war and eloquently expressed his belief in God as our great

Comforter. In a 1944 Easter prayer at Arlington National Cemetery General Marshall said:

Almighty God:

May those who have given their lives in the service of this nation rest in Thy care.

May those who are wounded in body find spiritual comfort under Thy guidance in the knowledge that through their sacrifice a great cause has been served.

May those who offer their lives in support of that cause, by land and sea and air, find strength in Thy divine guidance.

May those of us who serve this nation in its great purpose to secure freedom for all peoples be sustained by Thy blessing.

Give us strength, oh Lord, that we may be pure in heart and in purpose to the end that there may be peace on earth and good will among men.

[George C. Marshall Collection,
Speeches and statements]

To a friend, Mrs. Henry F. Meyer of Savannah, Georgia who had lost her husband a few years later, Marshall wrote his personal message of condolence.

December 21, 1953

My dear Mrs. Meyer:

Your note and the clippings reached me just before my departure for Oslo, from where I have just returned. It was very thoughtful of you to write and to send the clippings.

Mrs. Marshall and I understand and sympathize with your difficulty in adjusting to the loss of your husband. We—especially Mrs. Marshall—have experienced the sadness and emptiness occasioned by bereavements. Our greatest consolation has been in the love of those whom God has permitted to remain close to us and in the knowledge that His will is always wise and just.

Mrs. Marshall joins me in wishing you everything good in the New Year.

Faithfully yours,
George C. Marshall
[George C. Marshall Collection]

Dwight D. Eisenhower: Military and Moral Leader

Dwight D. Eisenhower (1890-1969) spent most of his life defending democracy. The third of seven sons raised in America's heartland, Eisenhower received a commission to West Point and made his career in the army. He served in staff assignments under the celebrated Generals Douglas MacArthur, John J. Pershing and Walter Krueger before America's entry into World War II. After Pearl Harbor, Eisenhower commanded the Allied Forces landing in North Africa. He helped orchestrate the invasion of Europe on D-Day, June 6, 1944 as Supreme Commander of the combined forces. A war hero of the first order, Eisenhower easily captured the Presidency in 1952 and steered the nation safely through the treacherous waters of the Cold War between the U.S. and the Soviet Union.

Eisenhower on Faith and Democracy

In a letter written during his first term to Retired General A.F. Lorenzen of Florida, President Eisenhower conveyed his deep belief that democracy depended upon religious faith to function properly.

" We hold that all men are endowed by their Creator with certain rights. The point is that except for this equality of right, a gift from the Almighty, there was no sense, logic or reason in free government."

Denver, Colorado
September 9, 1953

<u>Personal</u>

Dear General Lorenzen:

Thank you very much for forwarding to me the letter written by Father Athol Murray. I was most deeply interested in his observations, and, of course, more than complimented by his personal commendations.

Incidentally, I agree with him that liberty is not an absolute; yet it seems to me that in his statement he ignores the direct relationships between any form of free government and a deeply felt religious faith. When our forefathers attempted to express themselves and their ideas of government to the world, they were compelled to say, "We hold that all men are endowed by their Creator" with certain rights. The point is that except for this equality of right, a gift from the Almighty, there was no sense, logic or reason in free government. I think that any American contemplating the whole history of the writing of our Declaration and the establishment of our Constitution must conclude that an essential foundation stone of free government is this sincere religious faith.

Very sincerely,
Dwight D. Eisenhower
[Eisenhower, Dwight D.: Records as President (White House Central Files), 1953-1961]

216

A Search for Truth

A Eulogy to His Parents

Eisenhower was born in Texas just before the turn of the twentieth century and reared along with his six brothers in Abilene, Kansas. In a letter written during his first term as president to Mr. Archibald F. Bennett, he described his parents' godly influence on his life, and on his brothers' lives. At the heart of their family life was the instruction of God's holy Word.

The White House,
Washington, D.C., 1954
January 23

The Secretary of Agriculture tells me you would like to use a quotation regarding my parents on a program to be presented tomorrow. You are at liberty to use any part of the following, which is taken from a talk I made at the cornerstone laying of the Eisenhower Foundation, Abilene, Kansas, on June 4, 1952.

"My brothers and I devoutly believe in the extraordinary virtues of our parents. First of all they believed the admonition 'The fear of God is the beginning of all wisdom.' Their Bibles were a live and lusty influence in their lives. There was nothing sad about their religion. They believed in the Bible with happiness and contentment. They tried their best to instill the Bible, its doctrines, its beliefs, its convictions, in their sons. And they were frugal, possibly of necessity, because I have found out in later years that we were very poor, but the glory of America is that we didn't know it then. All that we knew was that our parents—of great courage—could say to us—opportunity is all about you. Reach out and take it. Do you want to go to school? Well, go. What are you afraid of? Do you have to stand around until someone comes along with a fat checkbook, and takes care of every possible care or difficulty you can have in that school? They didn't believe so. They were thrifty, they were economical, and they were honest.

"They were people of great courage, and I think they never stopped—they never had time—to hate or despise an enemy, or those that used them spitefully. They accepted their trials and tribulations and met them with courage and with never a thought of failure. They were a part and parcel of their community, of the philosophy that then governed our lives."

I request that if you do use any part of this, that you mention the date and circumstances of its delivery.

Dwight D. Eisenhower
[Eisenhower Papers as President, Name series, Box 15]

A Rewarder of Good Deeds

For Eisenhower, faith in God was a paramount aspect of life, the foundation of how people are to conduct their lives. During his first term as President (1953-1957), he wrote to a Brooklyn woman, Adelaide O'Mara, who made the news after she placed Ten Commandment cards in New York subways in the hope that they would draw people back to God.

A Search for Truth

August 6, 1956

<u>Personal and Confidential</u>

Dear Miss O'Mara:

With a real sense of personal uplift I read about the card containing The Ten Commandments that you placed in the BMT subway trains serving your area of New York City. The newspaper account reported you as saying that sometimes a small thing can change the world.

How right you are.

The world can well use an accumulation of good thoughts and good deeds, such as yours, which can call forth what Lincoln described as "the better angels of our nature." Despite the massive forces in motion in the world, it is still the individual person, believing in the right and doing good, that counts for most.

Certainly it is better to try to light a light than to bewail the darkness. For what you did, a personal "thank you."

Sincerely,
Dwight D. Eisenhower
[Eisenhower, Dwight D.; Papers as President, 1953-61; DDE Diary Series, Box 17, "Aug. 56 Misc. (4)"]

An Evangelist and His Critics

Billy Graham is one of the world's most recognizable Christians. Considered America's pastor, he also has been a friend of presidents and queens. Since 1947, he has preached the gospel of Jesus Christ to millions of people across the world through hundreds of evangelistic crusades, radio programs and television. The Holy Spirit has used Billy Graham to usher thousands upon thousands of souls into God's kingdom.

No one, however, not even Billy Graham, is without his critics. He has been castigated for not being sophisticated enough in his messages, for his closeness to presidents and, therefore, politics, and for his willingness to work with people from a wide variety of denominations.

In the spring of 1955 Graham preached in Scotland, drawing thousands in rallies covering three venues. That Good Friday he spoke on a BBC radio and TV broadcast about the meaning of the cross, a program that drew the largest audience since Queen Elizabeth II's coronation [Graham, p. 251]. The monarch was, in fact, part of that congregation and invited the American preacher to lead a private service at Windsor Castle.

Graham's ministry in Great Britain during that time was not without its detractors, though. A group of "fundamentalists" accused him of compromising the gospel by associating with Christian groups of which they disapproved. Graham's relationship with his wife, Ruth Bell Graham, helped him maintain his perspective. He says, "During this holy but hard time, letters to Ruth were my safety valve. In the intimacy of our partnership in the ministry, as well as our mutual love and respect, I could express myself to her as to few others" [Graham, p.

251]. In the following excerpts from letters to his wife, Graham expressed feelings about his ministry that he could share in the safety of their marital relationship.

"If this extreme type of fundamentalism was of God, it would have brought revival long ago. Instead, it has brought dissension, division, strife, and has produced dead and lifeless churches."

Some of the things they say are pure fabrications. . . . I do not intend to get down to their mud-slinging and get into endless arguments and discussions with them. . . . We are too busy winning souls to Christ and helping build the church to go down and argue with these . . . publicity-seekers. . . .

If a man accepts the deity of Christ and is living for Christ to the best of his knowledge, I intend to have fellowship with him in Christ. If this extreme type of fundamentalism was of God, it would have brought revival long ago. Instead, it has brought dissension, division, strife, and has produced dead and lifeless churches. . . .

You have no idea how lonesome it is without you! In thinking about my message tonight, I'd give anything if you were here to talk it over with. You are the only one that ever really understands my dilemma in the choice of messages. Your advice is the only one that I really trust. You have no idea how often I have listened to your advice and it has been as if it were spoken from the Lord. During the past year, I have learned to lean on you a great deal more than you realize. I'll be counting the days till you arrive.

[Graham, pp. 251-252]

Do Religion and Politics Mix?

In 1940 John F. Kennedy (1917-1963) gained national attention when his Harvard senior thesis became the best-selling While England Slept, a treatise about Great Britain's appeasement of Adolf Hitler. A war hero whose PT boat was severed by a Japanese destroyer in the South Pacific, Kennedy became a U.S. Congressman from Massachusetts in 1947. In 1953 that state's voters sent him to the Senate.

Kennedy achieved even greater recognition in 1956 when he garnered the Pulitzer Prize for his book, Profiles in Courage. Although he failed to secure the Democratic Vice-Presidential nomination that same year, JFK enlarged his political base. Many observers speculated about his future, sensing that he would make a bid for the Presidential nomination in 1960. This alarmed many Americans who feared the implications of having a Roman Catholic in the White House. What about the separation between Church and State? Would such a president come under the direct influence of the Pope?

Senator Kennedy received many letters from Americans who were concerned about his religious beliefs and how they might clash with his official duties. In early 1958 the Reverend Mickey R. Johnston, a Baptist pastor from Texas, wrote to JFK with some hard-hitting questions.

"How do your beliefs coincide with the traditional stand of the country on separation of church and state? . . . Where do you stand on the appointment of an American ambassador to the Vatican?"

16 January 1958

Dear Senator Kennedy:

It is with an open mind that I am writing you, for it does not seem Christian to actively oppose something until one can be certain of the stand to be taken. As you are constantly reminded many of the American people are opposed to your running for the Presidency because of your faith. It is not easy to forget that even today in many parts of the world our Baptist missionaries are being persecuted by the Roman Catholic Church.

However, to me it is still an individual matter, and begins with the person not the church. You have my deepest sympathy in this situation. You cannot hope to please everyone, and as a minister I am more than aware of that.

Can you answer some questions for me? I am Moderator of a group of Baptist Churches in this part of the State, and I cannot actively support or oppose anything either among the many churches or my own church without knowing more than I do.

The state of Texas is predominately Baptist, and the Editor of the Baptist newspaper for the entire state and I have discussed the possibility of your candidacy for the Presidency in 1960. It would seem to be all but a "lead-pipe cinch" that you will be the Democratic nominee.

Unless we Baptists know EXACTLY where you stand on major religious issues—we will be fighting your election down to the last inch.

If you would answer some questions that have been bothering me I would deeply appreciate it.

1. How do your beliefs coincide with the traditional stand of the country on separation of church and state?

2. Where do you stand on the appointment of an American ambassador to the Vatican?

February 5, 1958

Dear Reverend Johnston:

I am grateful to you for your letter of recent date and I welcome the opportunity to try to illustrate my position on the questions you have raised; for, like you, I feel that those of us who seek public office must be ready to express opinions on issues as we see them.

In the first place, I believe that the position of the Catholic Church with respect to the question of separation of church and state has been greatly distorted and is very much misunderstood in this country. As a matter of fact, I am quite convinced that there is no traditional or uniformly held view on the subject. For my own part, I thoroughly subscribe to the principles embodied in the Constitution on this point, particularly those contained in the First Amendment. It is my belief that the American Constitution wisely refrains from involvement with any organized religion, considering this most important but personal sphere not an area for government intervention. To this view I subscribe without reservation.

I do not favor the establishment of diplomatic relations with the Vatican, for I do not perceive any particular advantage to the United States in sending an ambassador there—and it is my belief that this should be the criterion in deciding on diplomatic relations.

I have no hesitancy in saying to you that in my public life I act according to my own conscience and on the basis of my own judgment, without reference to any other authority. As a public official I have no obligation to any private institution, religious or otherwise. My obligation is to the good of all.

On the question of aid to private schools, my position is also unequivocal. I support the Constitution without reservation, and as I understand its principles it forbids aid to private institutions. In this respect you may be interested to see the attached copy of a bill which I have recently introduced to provide Federal aid for the construction of public schools.

I appreciate the good faith in which your letter was written and I hope that my reply will help to clarify my position.

> With every good wish,
> Sincerely yours,
> John F. Kennedy
> [John Fitzgerald Kennedy Library]

An Exchange of Telegrams

Kennedy ran for the Presidency in 1960 and won, defeating Republican Richard M. Nixon in the nationwide election. The youngest president and first Roman Catholic

*to be elected in American history, Kennedy kept mainly to
himself about his personal religious beliefs. He did, however, maintain a cordial relationship with Pope John the
Twenty-third, just as he did with many world leaders. They
exchanged telegrams at the occasion of Kennedy's inaugu-
ration.*

Cittadelvaticano 1850
20 Jan 1961

As Your Excellency assumes the honerous duties
and responsibilities of the Presidency of the United
States of America we extend to you anew our sincere
felicitations and we prayerfully invoke upon you the
abiding assistance of Almighty God.

Johannes XXIII PP

1961 Feb. 2

Your Holiness:

I deeply appreciate your message on the occasion
of my assumption of the office of President of the
United States. Your good wishes and prayers are a
source of encouragement and inspiration as I take
up the duties and responsibilities of the Presidency.

Sincerely,
John F. Kennedy
[John Fitzgerald Kennedy Library]

Letter from a Birmingham Jail

The Rev. Dr. Martin Luther King, Jr. (1929-1968) first came to the nation's attention in 1955. Rosa Parks had just refused to give up her seat to a white man on a Montgomery, Alabama bus, a step that resulted in a year-long bus boycott to promote desegregation. Leading that protest was the Dexter Avenue Baptist Church's twenty-six-year-old pastor. He was so successful in organizing and inspiring that city's black population that when his fellow pastors organized the Southern Christian Leadership Conference to combat racial prejudice, they elected King its first president.

In 1963 the young minister rose to even greater prominence when he organized a massive civil rights campaign in Birmingham, Alabama, as well as voter registration drives, and those to promote desegregation, better housing and education for blacks across the South. In August, he gave the most famous speech of his career, "I Have a Dream," during the March on Washington. He was arrested three times that year alone. During his stint in a Birmingham jail, he wrote these ringing words to his fellow clergy about brotherhood and the responsibility of the Church to combat injustice.

"Injustice anywhere is a threat to justice everywhere. We are caught in an inescapable network of mutuality, tied in a single garment of destiny."

April 16, 1963

My Dear Fellow Clergy:

While confined here in the Birmingham city jail, I came across your recent statement calling my present activities "unwise and untimely." Seldom do I pause to answer criticism of my work and ideas. If I sought to answer all the criticisms that cross my desk, my secretaries would have little time for anything other than such correspondence in the course of the day, and I would have no time for constructive work. But since I feel that you are men of genuine good will and that your criticisms are sincerely set forth, I want to try to answer your statements in what I hope will be patient and reasonable terms. . . .

I am in Birmingham because injustice is here. Just as the prophets of the eighth century B.C. left their villages and carried their "thus saith the Lord" far beyond the boundaries of their home towns, and just as the Apostle Paul left his village of Tarsus and carried the gospel of Jesus Christ to the far corners of the Greco-Roman world, so am I compelled to carry the gospel of freedom beyond my own home town. Like Paul, I must constantly respond to the Macedonian call for aid. . . .

Meanwhile, I am cognizant of the interrelatedness of all communities and states. I cannot sit idly by in Atlanta and not be concerned about what happens in Birmingham. Injustice anywhere is a threat to justice everywhere. We are caught in an inescapable network of mutuality, tied in a single garment of destiny. Whatever affects one directly, affects all indirectly. Never again can we afford to live with the narrow, provincial "outside agitator" idea. Anyone who lives inside the United States can never be considered an outsider anywhere within its bounds.

I must make two honest confessions to you, my Christian and Jewish brothers. First, I must confess that over the past few years I have been gravely disappointed with the white moderate. I have almost reached the regrettable conclusion that the Negro's great stumbling block in his stride toward freedom is not the White Citizen's Counciler or the Ku Klux Klanner, but the white moderate, who is more devoted to "order" than to justice; who prefers a negative peace which is the absence of tension to a positive peace which is the presence of justice; who constantly says: "I agree with you in the goal you seek, but I cannot agree with your methods of direct action." who [sic] paternalistically believes he can set the timetable for another man's freedom who lives by a mythical concept of time and who constantly advises the Negro to wait for a "more convenient season." Shallow understanding from people of good will is more frustrating than absolute misunderstanding from people of ill will. Lukewarm acceptance is much more bewildering than outright rejection. . . .

I had hoped that the white moderate would understand that law and order exist for the purpose of establishing justice and that when they fan in this purpose they become the dangerously structured dams that block the flow of social progress. I had hoped that the white moderate would understand that the present tension in the South is a necessary phase of the transition from an obnoxious negative peace, in which the Negro passively accepted his unjust plight, to a substantive and positive peace, in which all men will respect the dignity and worth of human personality. Actually, we who engage in nonviolent direct action are not the creators of tension. We merely bring to the surface the hidden tension that is already alive. We bring it out in the open, where it can be seen and dealt with. Like a boil that can never be cured so long as it is covered up but must be opened with its ugliness to the natural medicines of air and light, injustice must be exposed, with all the tension its exposure creates, to the light of human conscience and the air of national opinion before it can be cured. . . .

But though I was initially disappointed at being categorized as an extremist, as I continued to think about the matter I gradually gained a measure of satisfaction from the label. Was not Jesus an extremist for love: "Love your enemies, bless them that curse you, do good to them that hate you, and pray for them which despitefully use you, and persecute you." Was not Amos an extremist for justice: "Let justice roll down like waters and righteousness like an ever-flowing stream." Was not Paul an extremist for the Christian gospel: "I bear in my body the marks of the Lord Jesus." Was not Martin Luther an extremist: "Here I stand; I can not do otherwise, so help me God." And John Bunyan: "I will stay in jail to the end of my days before I make a butchery of my conscience." And Abraham Lincoln: "This nation cannot survive half slave and half free." And Thomas Jefferson: "We hold these truths to be self-evident, that all men are created equal. . . . " So the question is not whether we will be extremists, but what kind of extremists we will be. . . .

I have traveled the length and breadth or Alabama, Mississippi and all the other southern states. On sweltering summer days and crisp autumn mornings I have looked at the South's beautiful churches with their lofty spires pointing heavenward. I have beheld the impressive outlines of her massive religious-education buildings. Over and over I have found myself asking: "What kind of people worship here? Who is their God? Where were their voices when the lips of Governor Barnett dripped with words of interposition and nullification? Where were they when Governor Wallace gave a clarion call for defiance and hatred? Where were their voices of support when bruised and weary Negro men and women decided to rise from the dark dungeons of complacency to the bright hills of creative protest?"

Yes, these questions are still in my mind. In deep disappointment I have wept over the laxity of the church. But be assured that my tears have been tears of love. There can be no deep disappointment where there is not deep love. Yes, I love the church. How could I do otherwise? I am in the rather unique position of being the son, the grandson and the great-grandson of preachers. Yes, I see the church as the body of Christ. But, oh! How we have blemished and scarred that body through social neglect and through fear of being nonconformists. . . .

There was a time when the church was very powerful in the time when the early Christians rejoiced at being deemed worthy to suffer for what they believed. In those days the church was not merely a thermometer that recorded the ideas and principles of popular opinion; it was a thermostat that transformed the mores of society. Whenever the early Christians entered a town, the people in power became disturbed and immediately sought to convict the Christians for being "disturbers of the peace" and "outside agitators." But the Christians pressed on, in the conviction that they were "a colony of heaven" called to obey God rather than man. Small in number, they were big in commitment. They were too God intoxicated to be "astronomically intimidated." By their effort and example they brought an end to such ancient evils as infanticide and gladiatorial contests.

Things are different now. So often the contemporary church is a weak, ineffectual voice with an uncertain sound. So often it is an archdefender of the status quo. Far from being disturbed by the presence of the church, the power structure of the average community is consoled by the church's silent and often even vocal sanction of things as they are.

But the judgment of God is upon the church as never before. If today's church does not recapture the sacrificial spirit of the early church, it will lose its authenticity, forfeit the loyalty of millions, and be dismissed as an irrelevant social club with no meaning for the twentieth century. Every day I meet young people whose disappointment with the church has turned into outright disgust. . . .

I hope the church as a whole will meet the challenge of this decisive hour. But even if the church does not come to the aid of justice, I have no despair about the future. I have no fear about the outcome of our struggle in Birmingham, even if our motives are at present misunderstood. We will reach the goal of freedom in Birmingham, and all over the nation, because the goal of America is freedom. Abused and scorned though we may be, our destiny is tied up with America's destiny. Before the pilgrims landed at Plymouth, we were here. Before the pen of Jefferson etched the majestic words of the Declaration of Independence across the pages of history, we were here. For more than two centuries our forebears labored in this country without wages; they made cotton king; they built the homes of their masters while suffering gross injustice and shameful humiliation—and yet out of a bottomless vitality they continued to thrive and develop. If the inexpressible cruelties of slavery could not stop us, the opposition we now face will surely fail. We will win our freedom because the sacred heritage of our nation and the eternal will of God are embodied in our echoing demands. . . .

> Yours for the cause of
> Peace and Brotherhood.
> Martin Luther King, Jr.

[King, p. 9]

God on Campus

College campuses across the United States throbbed with rebellion in 1970. Many students banged the drums of free sex, radical feminism, experimental drugs, eastern religions and acid rock. Others who had grown up in prosperity rejected materialism, decrying the poverty and destitution of millions. Newspapers carried stories of their disquietude, telling the nation and the world how upset many young people were about those issues and more—pollution, consumer waste, racism, the threat of nuclear war and the assassinations of their heroes. Of all the causes that college students took up, however, none was more fervently adopted than protesting the war in Vietnam with its fuzzy boundaries and vague rationale. At many colleges and universities students arranged "sit-in" demonstrations which often brought the business of college administrations to a standstill.

Not all students revolted against their elders and the "establishment," however. The most vocal and dramatic ones were, in fact, a minority. Many other college students were undergoing a transformation of a different kind, one that left them engaged in a profound relationship with Jesus Christ. Nowhere was this more visible than at a small Methodist college near Lexington, Kentucky when God set the campus aflame with His presence in February, 1970.

On a cold and windy day, 1,000 Asburians gathered for 10 a.m. chapel in Hughes Auditorium, seated according to their classes. The dean had been scheduled to preach, but at the last minute he decided to give a personal testimony about God's activity in his life. Then he *invited a few students to share what the Lord was doing with them.*

Several students stepped to the platform to tell heartfelt stories of God's personal grace. As they spoke, a sense of God's presence pervaded the auditorium. The end of the chapel period came and one professor called any students who wanted to pray to come forward. Unexpectedly, a mass of Asburians thronged toward the front as everyone sang "Just As I Am." The bell rang for classes to begin, but it went unheeded as students began publicly to confess their sins. Reconciliations took place between those who harbored bitter feelings toward each other.

By noon, the chapel service was still going strong. One professor went to the cafeteria for a department meeting only to discover that the place was nearly deserted. He headed over to Hughes to find out why chapel hadn't ended.

The college's administration cancelled the rest of the day's classes, and almost all of the 1,550 seats in Hughes were filled as the service lasted into that evening. One student reported losing track of time with no sense of hunger, thirst or other physical needs.

The revival spread across the street to Asbury Seminary the next day during its scheduled chapel service. Many townspeople from Wilmore crammed Hughes Auditorium. As the nonstop service continued into the rest of the week, several local pastors urged their flocks to attend the revival rather than their own church services that Sunday.

Finally on February 10, a full week after the revival began, the Asbury administration resumed classes at the end of that day's chapel period. They would, however, keep Hughes open for prayer and nightly meetings. God's campus "sit-in" had lasted 185 hours.

An Asbury student sent this letter to the editor of her hometown paper, The Citizen-Patriot, Jackson, Michigan:

"[Asbury College students] plan to turn the world upside-down, not because they're troublemakers, but for the sake of Jesus Christ! They want to go to other campuses—not to cause a riot but to share the spirit of revival!"

Dear Editor:

There is a new kind of demonstration at Asbury during these days of national college sit-ins—not in the administration offices, but in the college and seminary chapels. Students are throwing around a lot of three-, four-, and five-letter words, too. Words like "joy," "love," "pray," and "faith."

They plan to turn the world upside-down, not because they're troublemakers, but for the sake of Jesus Christ! They want to go to other campuses—not to cause a riot but to share the spirit of revival! The demonstration is a demonstration of faith. It is not getting out-of-hand for it is God's hand.

[Coleman, p. 89]

Revival Fire Spreads

The revival's wide-reaching effects spread far beyond Wilmore to other campuses throughout the nation, and on to the world at large. This happened wherever Asbury students testified to the remarkable revival during the following months. Newspapers were filled with accounts of this glorious unfolding of God's presence, and several wrote letters about the revival.

From the Anderson College Newspaper:

Dear Editor:

The Revival is a spiritual phenomenon of integrity. This happening has given to hundreds of students an experience of genuine spiritual value. Counseling sessions with students have convinced me this happening has been deeper than mere emotion. Some students have at last entered into true and worthy commitments. Scores of others now have adopted proper standards for their lives. Christian beliefs have become important—and redemptive. The attitudes of many students have become less censorious and more meaningfully centered and controlled. I have heard many confessions that let me know that prejudices are being examined and released. The Revival has helped students to relate love to logic, feeling to facts and faith to reason.

James Massey, Chaplain

[Coleman, p. 75]

A Search for Truth

From a Chicago-Tribune *reporter on April 12, 1970:*

The revival has made a splash that is sending ripples throughout the country. Nobody can recall a similar church-related event that has drawn this kind of response in Anderson [College]. Many people who came prepared to be skeptical at the emotional nature of the meetings have been impressed with the sincerity and the contagious atmosphere of the sessions. . . . In a day when many congregations are worried about losing their appeal to young people, Anderson's "Revival of Love" seems to be saying something.

[Coleman, p. 75]

A People's President

President Ronald Reagan (1911-), who was known as "the Great Communicator," developed his captivating speaking style after graduating from Eureka College and taking a job as a radio sports announcer.

Over the years, Reagan developed political experience that eventually helped him gain the California governorship in 1966. He served in that position until 1975. A spokesman for conservative principles, Reagan captured the nation's support in the 1980 presidential election. Just a little over two months after taking the oath of office, he nearly died in an assassination attempt. Reagan's popularity swelled because of the grace and sense of humor he exhibited during that crisis, especially his message to wife Nancy, "Honey, I forgot to duck." He also quipped that he hoped the doctors were Republicans.

Reagan's popularity and political success originated from a genuine concern for people. Shortly after the assassination attempt, a presidential staffer entered the President's hospital room and was distressed to find that he wasn't there. Upon closer examination, he discovered Reagan kneeling in the bathroom where he was wiping the floor. The President explained that he had spilled some water and didn't want to bother the all-too-busy nurses about it.

A Stand for Freedom of Speech

In the late 1980's a high school senior named Angela became her class's valedictorian. She wanted to make mention in her speech of the importance of God in her life, but school authorities forbade her to do so. White

House domestic policy aide Gary Bauer heard about her dilemma and brought it to President Reagan's attention. According to Reagan speech writer Peggy Noonan, Bauer's colleagues tittered in embarrassment. "Here they were assembled in the White House, ready to talk about serious things like the Soviets, and here's poor Gary telling him about some little kid . . ." [p. 250].

A reproachful glance from the president quieted the room, and Bauer continued. He told the president he thought there was something vitally wrong in our country when an American child could not speak in a public school setting about the importance of religious faith in her life. He reminded Reagan that the girl only wanted to do what the president did in speeches all the time. Everyone knew he was right.

The president was touched and asked if there was something he could do about the situation. Bauer suggested meeting Angela, or writing to her. The president sent the teenager a letter.

"I know that it is often difficult to stand up for one's beliefs when they are being harshly challenged. But . . . personal faith and conviction are strengthened, not weakened, in adversity."

Dear Angela,

I read of the events surrounding your proposed commencement address with considerable interest. Like you, I have long believed in the paramount importance of faith in God.

Angela, your actions on behalf of your religious convictions demonstrate not only the strength and passion of those convictions, but your admirable personal courage in facing those who have challenged you. I know that it is often difficult to stand up for one's beliefs when they are being harshly challenged. But as one who has seen many challenges over a long lifetime, I can assure you that personal faith and conviction are strengthened, not weakened, in adversity.

Nancy and I wish you well throughout your life. God bless you.

Ronald Reagan

[Noonan, pp. 249-251]

Cheerful Optimism

Among the occupants of the White House known for their cheerful optimism, Theodore and Franklin Roosevelt and Ronald Reagan immediately come to mind.

Reagan left office in 1989 after two terms, but his sense of optimism about the future continued to impact the American people. In the fall of 1994 he learned that he suffered from Alzheimer's disease. Reagan promptly wrote a letter in his own hand to the American people, telling them in his uniquely sanguine way about his malady. It expressed his confidence that while he was approaching the end of his life, the nation he loved and served faced a shining future.

Nov. 5, 1994

My Fellow Americans,

I have recently been told that I am one of the millions of Americans who will be afflicted with Alzheimer's Disease.

Upon learning this news, Nancy and I had to decide whether as private citizens we would keep this a private matter or whether we would make this news known in a public way.

In the past Nancy suffered from breast cancer and I had my cancer surgeries. We found through our open disclosures we were able to raise public awareness. We were happy that as a result many more people underwent testing. They were treated in early stages and able to return to normal, healthy lives.

So now, we feel it is important to share it with you. In opening our hearts, we hope this might promote greater awareness of this condition. Perhaps it will encourage a clearer understanding of the individuals and families who are affected by it.

At the moment I feel just fine. I intend to live the remainder of the years God gives me on this earth doing the things I have always done. I will continue to share life's journey with my beloved Nancy and my family. I plan to enjoy the great outdoors and stay in touch with my friends and supporters.

Unfortunately, as Alzheimer's Disease progresses, the family often bears a heavy burden. I only wish there was some way I could spare Nancy from this painful experience. When the time comes I am confident that with your help she will face it with faith and courage.

In closing let me thank you, the American people for giving me the great honor of allowing me to serve as your President. When the Lord calls me home whenever that may be, I will leave with the greatest love for this country of ours and eternal optimism for its future.

I now begin the journey that will lead me into the sunset of my life. I know that for America there will always be a bright dawn ahead.

Thank you my friends. May God always bless you.

Sincerely,
Ronald Reagan
[Davis, Patti, p. 123]

Bibliography
&
Topical Index

Bibliography

Ammerman, E.H. Jim. *After the Storm*. Nashville: Star Song Communications, 1991.

Armstrong, Kerry. Chickasaw Historical Research Page: http://www.flash.net/~kma/.

Bartlett, John. *Bartlett's Familiar Quotations*, Sixteenth Edition. Boston: Little, Brown and Company, 1992.

Basler, Roy P., ed. *Abraham Lincoln: His Speeches and Writings*. Cleveland, OH: World Publishing Company, 1946.

Baym, Nina, ed., et al. *The Norton Anthology of American Literature*. New York: W.W. Norton and Company, 1995.

Ira Berlin, et al. "Family and Freedom: Black Families in the American Civil War." *American History, Volume I: Pre-colonial Through Reconstruction*. Ed. Robert James Maddox. Guilford, CT: The Dushkin Publishing Group, Inc, 1989.

BGC Archives. Box 38, folder 10, Collection 318. Wheaton, IL.

Cappon, Lester J. *The Adams-Jefferson Letters*. Chapel Hill, NC: University of North Carolina Press, 1959.

Churchill, Winston. *Their Finest Hour*. New York: Bantam Books, 1949.

The Civil War. Copyright 1990 Public Broadcasting Station.

Coleman, Robert E., ed. *One Divine Moment*. Old Tappan, NJ: Fleming H. Revell Company, 1970.

Cousins, Norman. *In God We Trust: the Religious Beliefs and Ideas of the American Founding Fathers*. New York: Harper and Brothers Publishers, 1958.

Davis, Burke. *They Called Him Stonewall*. New York: The Fairfax Press, 1954.

Great Letters in American History

Davis, Jefferson. *The Papers of Jefferson Davis*, Vol. 7. Baton Rouge, LA: Louisiana State University Press, 1971.

Davis, Patti. *Angels Don't Die: My Father's Gift of Faith*. New York: HarperCollins Publishers, Inc., 1995. (10 East 53rd St., NY, 10022).

Dunn, Mary Maples and Dunn, Richard S. *The Papers of William Penn*: Volume One, 1644-1679. Philadelphia, PA: University of Pennsylvania Press, 1981.

Eisenhower, Dwight D.: Records as President (White House Central Files), 1953-61; Official File, Box 429, "OF 102 Govt. of the U.S. (1)." Used by permission of John Eisenhower.

Eisenhower, Dwight D.: Papers as President. Name series, Box 15, "Genealogy (2)." Used by permission of John Eisenhower.

Eisenhower, Dwight D.: Papers as President, 1953-61; DDE Diary Series, Box 17, "Aug. 56 Misc. (4)." Used by permission of John Eisenhower.

Farley, Alan. "Reports from the Actual Chaplains and What They Saw." *The Christian Banner* XIII (April/May/June/July 1997): 13-14.

Howe, Julia Ward. Appeal to Womanhood Throughout the World [online]. Available http://www.cs.cmu.edu/~mmbt/women/richards/howe/howe-I-XIV.html

Furnas, J.C. *The Americans*. New York: G.P. Putnam's Sons, 1969.

George C. Marshall Collection, Box 1, Folder 35. The George C. Marshall Foundation, Lexington, Virginia.

General Douglas MacArthur Foundation, MacArthur Square, Norfolk, Virginia.

Graham, Billy. *Just As I Am*. San Francisco: HarperCollins, 1997.

Bibliography

Grant, George. *The Blood of the Moon*. Brentwood, TN: Wolgemuth & Hyatt, Publishers, Inc., 1991.

Herrnstadt, Richard L., ed. *The Letters of A. Bronson Alcott*. Ames, IA: The Iowa State University Press, 1969.

Holzer, Harold, Editor. *Dear Mr. Lincoln: Letters to the President*. Reading, MA: Addison-Wesley Publishing Company, 1993.

[Online]. Available http://www.clpgh.org/ein/andrcarn/acgrantone.html.

Janney, Rebecca Price. *Great Women in American History*. Camp Hill, PA: Horizon Books, 1996.

John Fitzgerald Kennedy Library; Religious Issues File.

King, Martin Luther, Jr. "Letter from Birmingham Jail, April 16, 1963." *Loaves and Fishes* 17 (January-February, 1998): 9.

Levin, Phyllis Lee. *Abigail Adams: A Biography*. New York, NY: St. Martin's Press, 1987.

Marshall, Catherine. *To Live Again*. New York, NY: Avon Books, 1957. (The Hearst Corporation, 959 Eighth Ave., NY, 10019)

McCallum, James Dow, ed. *The Letters of Eleazar Wheelock's Indians*. Hanover, NH: Dartmouth College Publications, 1932.

Moran, Philip R., ed. *Ulysses S. Grant: 1822-1885*. Dobbs Ferry, NY: Oceana Publications, Inc., 1968.

National Park Service, George Washington Carver National Monument, Diamond, MO.

Noonan, Peggy. *What I Saw at the Revolution*. New York: Ivy Books, 1990.

Parton, James, et al. *Eminent Women of the Age*. Hartford, CT: S.M. Betts and Company, 1869.

Perry, John. *Sgt. York: His Life, Legend and Legacy*. Nashville, TN: Broadman and Holman Publishers, 1997.

Quinn, David B. and Alison M., eds. *The First Colonists: Documents on the Planting of the First English Settlements in North America 1584-1590*. Raleigh, NC: North Carolina Department of Cultural Resources Division of Archives and History, 1982.

Reuther, Rosemary Radford, and Keller, Rosemary Skinner, eds. *Women and Religion in America*, Vol. 2. San Francisco: Harper and Row, Publishers, 1983.

Roosevelt, Theodore. *Foes of Our Own Household*. New York: Charles Scribner's Sons, 1917, p. 3.

Rosenman, Samuel I. *The Public Papers and Addresses of Franklin D. Roosevelt*, Vol. 4. New York: Random House, 1938-50.

Ruchames, Louis. *The Abolitionists: A Collection of Their Writings*. New York, NY: Capricorn Books, 1963.

Schuster, M. Lincoln. *A Treasury of the World's Great Letters*. New York: Simon and Schuster, 1940.

Turner, Charles W. *Letters from the Stonewall Brigade*. Berryville, VA: Rockbridge Publishing Company, 1992.

Unger, Irwin. *These United States*. Englewood Cliffs, NJ: Prentice Hall, 1995.

Vanauken, Sheldon. *A Severe Mercy*. New York: Harper and Row, 1977.

Washington, George. *Writings*. New York: Penguin Books, 1997.

Wirt, William. *The Life and Character of Patrick Henry*. Philadelphia, PA: Porter and Coates, n.d.

Topical Index

Topical Index

Topical Index

Other Books by
Rebecca Price Janney

Great Stories in American History
(Adult non-fiction)

Great Women in American History
(Adult non-fiction)

The Impossible Dreamers Series
(Children's historic adventure series)

The Heather Reed Mystery Series
(Children's mystery series)

Harriet Tubman